Towards World Government

The New World Order

by

Deirdre Manifold

Printed by Standard Printed Products Ltd., Galway

* * * * *

Firinne Publications
15 Dalysfort Road, Galway

to
all the brave writers
living and dead
who have made
this book possible

Contents

Preface 1

The Illuminati 3

The Media 6

The Family Farm 9

Our Children 10

The Left and the Right 15

The U.S.A 17

The New Age 26

The Catholic Church and Freemasonry 29

Psychopolitics 35

Rakovsky 49

The Merger...103

The Woman of Genesis..................................109

Postscript...123

Bibliography 125

Preface

One of our most respected historians has said that power corrupts and that absolute power corrupts absolutely. The struggle for absolute power over the whole human race is now at its zenith. This is war on all fronts, not just political or economic. Our war is against Principalities and Powers, and humanly speaking, we haven't a chance. However not only have we a chance, we are already on the winning side once we understand the nature of the warfare. It began in the Garden of Eden when God said: "I will put enmity between thee and the Woman, between your seed and her seed. She will crush your head and you will lie in wait for her heel." Gen. 3.15.

Rakovsky has given a brilliant exposition of the manner in which the warfare is being conducted in the political and economic field. If it were not first and last a spiritual warfare there would scarcely be need to say more, for Rakovsky would have said it all. But life on this earth is only a drop in the ocean of eternity. We are above all spiritual beings made for an eternal destiny. What follows is an attempt to look at the total war that is afoot in its true perspective, and to bring to the notice of interested people the plans that are afoot to bring about total world slavery from which the planners intend there will be no escape. Herein is given a graphic but reasonably comprehensive view of what is going on behind the scenes towards this end. To succeed it has got to be pursued surreptitiously and the end and motives vehemently denied. But the evidence is all there. It is made up of undeniable facts of history. Call it a jigsaw puzzle, the pieces being the titles in the bibliography at the end of this book. Strange you never heard of most of them and the chances are you won't be able to find any of them in your local bookshop, no matter how well stocked.

The key to the riddle is, of course, money, and the power of the masters who issue it and control its spending. As Rakovsky has said, and he knew, "money is power, the only power." That power is now becoming absolute and when that day dawns, which may be sooner than we think, it says in Revelations Chapter 13, 15-18.

> *"And he had power to give life unto the image of the beast, that the image of the beast should both speak, and cause that as many as would not worship the image of the beast should be killed.*
>
> *And he caused all, both small and great, rich and poor, free and bond, to receive a mark in their right hand, or in their foreheads: And no man might buy or sell, save he that had the mark, or the name of the beast, or the number of his name.*
>
> *Here is wisdom. Let him that hath understanding count the number of the beast: for it is the number of a man: and his number is six hundred three score and six."*

The age of technology has now reached a point sufficiently sophisticated to make this prophesy a reality. More than likely it will not come in the next century. It may come in what is left of this one.

CHAPTER 1

The Illuminati

> *"And Jesus was led by the Spirit into the wilderness*
> *And the devil, taking him up into a high mountain, showed him all the kingdoms of the world in a moment of time. And the devil said unto him: All these I will give thee and the glory of them if thou wilt bow down and adore me....*
> *And Jesus answering said.... 'Thou shalt not tempt the Lord thy God.'"*
>
> Luke Chapter 4. 1-12.
>
> *"We shall have world government whether or not you like it, by conquest or consent."*
>
> Paul Warburg to the U.S. senate on 17.2.1953

While the war began in Eden it was not until the 1770's that a plan was formulated to bring about the subjection of the whole human race to an oligarchy of evil men. There was established on May 1, 1776, a group known as the Illuminati by one Adam Wesshaupt, a University Professor employed by the family of Rothschilds to give form and precision to their plan for World Government. It was the first time in history that it was claimed that the end justified the means.

The aims of the Illuminati were to destroy all ordered government, all Kings and Altars, The King had to go because he protected the altar.

Weishaupt recruited some 2,000 paid followers, who would be promised success in this life even if they did not live to see World Government. These included some of the most intelligent in the fields of letters, education, the sciences, finance and industry. They were to be given a rigorous training, and, if, after a trial period, some members did not show signs of being capable of corruption they were dropped from the society.

Monetary and sex bribery were to be used to control men already in high places of government and other fields of endeavour; Universities and Colleges of Education were to be infiltrated in order to cultivate students of exceptional mental ability, belonging to well bred families, who would be recommended for special training in internationalism. Such training would be provided by granting scholarships to those selected illuminists.

The plans were discovered and passed to the Bavarian Government, when a messenger carrying their plans, was killed in an electric storm. Neighbouring Governments were warned, but their agents were now so firmly entrenched behind the scenes they were able to have the warnings ignored. The Bavarian Government immediately banned the Society. It went underground, moved into France, where it embarked on a take-over of the Masonic Lodges, and by means of that infiltration brought about the French Revolution, its first giant step on the road to world rule. How did they achieve such phenomenal success in so short a time?

Influential people who submitted to their control, plus the students specially selected and trained, were to be used as Agents and placed behind the scenes of all governments as experts and specialists to advise the top executives to adopt policies which in the long run would serve the secret plans of the Illuminati, One World Government.

Perhaps the most vital directive of Weishaupt's plan was to obtain absolute control of the Press, so that all news and information could be slanted to convince the masses that a One

World Government is the only solution to our many and varied problems, and the only road to peace in this world. Control the channels of information he insisted. Then you will have control of men's minds, with all that this entails.

In America the Council of Foreign Relations which has, in effect, ruled that country for most of this century at its higher esoteric level, and judging by its actions, is believed to be the Illuminati of today. It has sister Councils in most European countries, all of one mind that world government is the only solution to our problems and the sure road to peace. Peace is the carrot held before the world's dumb donkeys.

> *"My people are destroyed for lack of knowledge: because thou hast rejected knowledge, I will also reject thee.... seeing thou hast forgotten the law of thy God, I will also forget thy children."*
> *Hosea Chapter 4.6.*

Chapter 2

The Media

John Swinton, one-time editor of the New York Times, in reply to a toast "An Independent Press," at a banquet given in his honour in New York on his retirement made the following statement:

> *"What folly is this toasting an independent press? Everyone present here tonight knows there is no such thing as an independent press. You know it and I know it. There is not one of you who would dare to write his honest opinions, and if he did, you know beforehand it would never appear in print. I am paid 250 dollars a week to keep my honest opinions out of the paper I am connected with. Others of you are paid similar salaries for similar work. The business of the journalist is to destroy the Truth, to lie outright, to pervert, to vilify, to fawn at the foot of mammon, and to sell himself, his country and his race for his daily bread. You know this, and I know it, and what folly it is to be toasting an independent press! We are the tools and vassals of rich men behind the scenes. We are jumping jacks – they pull the strings and we dance. Our talents, our possibilities and our lives are the property of these men. We are intellectual prostitutes."*

The above quotation is striking proof of the extent of the success of the Illuminati in controlling the channels of information. Money is power, the only power, as Rakovsky has said, and that power is used to control the Media. The intellectual prostitution business can only belong to the super rich.

No king or emperor of old, no conquering Napoleon, ever disposed of a power even remotely approaching that of a handful of individuals who control America's mass media. Their power reaches not only into every home in America, but into nearly every home in the English speaking world. It is the power which shapes and moulds the minds of virtually every citizen, young or old, rich or poor, simple or sophisticated. News is managed and what is today termed as 'entertainment' is managed in the same way as news, and in this both subtlety and thoroughness are exercised.

The way in which the news is covered, which items are emphasised and which are played down, the reporter's choice of words, and the commentator's tone of voice, the choice of headline and illustration, all of these profoundly affect our thinking.

Virtually all national and international T.V. news in the U.S., is filmed, edited and broadcast by just three Corporations, ABC, CBS and NBC. Each of these three has been under the absolute control of one man over a long enough period of time - ranging from 32 to 57 years - for him to staff the corporation at every level with officers of his own choosing and thus to place his imprint indelibly upon it.

The same tight Illuminati control is held over the big newspaper world as in the T.V. and Radio world.

The book publishing business is somewhat different. There are very many courageous Americans who invest in the publishing of books that tell it how it is, but the message gets to no more than a small minority, who have no power in the political or economic sense. The reason is that the distribution of books, as well as magazines, is in the hands of the same monopolists. If, between five and ten per cent of the public, happens to know what is going on, it is about as much. They are ridiculed by the Media if they get a mention at all, mostly such books get the silent treatment, but if they do get a mention it is only to fling personal abuse at the authors.

It requires genius to convince nearly a quarter billion Americans that they are taxed to the hilt to pay for an army and arms to fight something called Communism, while all the time their Government has been foisting this terrible system on nation after nation, since it first ensured that it was successful in the U.S.S.R. It cannot be explained rationally. The answer is in the supernatural.

CHAPTER 3

The Family Farm

In the United States a family farm is sold up every six minutes. In 1950 there were seven and a half million family farms. By 1987 this figure was reduced to two and a half million. A Farmers Magazine called **Acres U.S.A.** states that it has on file a letter from the Federal Reserve Bank stating that it was hoped this figure will be reduced to 100,000 by 1995. If this happens it will be the greatest disaster in history.

In The Irish Times of March 2, 1990, we are told that since joining the European Community, Ireland has lost one-thind of its farmers, and today one in four farm families live below the poverty line.

Britain's farming workforce fell by 13,000 last year, one of the steepest in the decade, according to goverment figures issued yesterday.

When directors and farm owners are counted the fall was even steeper with 14,000 fewer people overall earning a living from the land in 1989

Irish Independent Wed. Feb. 7th'90

The proportion of people leaving the land in Canada, Australia and New Zealand is roughly the same.

Does anyone really believe that this is just happening. It is happening because it has been made to happen. The reason can hardly be plainer. The issue is freedom. The aim is control, people control. In cities and even in towns control is easy. On the land man is free.

"With land a man is a king
Without it he is nothing"

Playwright John B. Keane.

CHAPTER 4

Our Children

They are after our children

The war is on all fronts, but nowhere is it more ruthlessly waged than on our children. They are no longer safe in the womb. An animal will fight to the death for its offspring. Why? Was not that instinct planted there by its Creator. The animal has only its instinct. Man has free will and instinct.

Any emotionally disturbed woman fed by propaganda may commit the unspeakable crime of murdering her own child while still in the womb. God is for ever a forgiving God. If she repents she will be forgiven. But what of the men and women, not so disturbed, who sit around in Parliament and deliberately plan the murder not like Herod of a number in a certain place under two years of age, but of millions and millions of the most defenceless of all humankind.

And then for those children who do see the light of day the directives of the Illuminati, who richly rewarded Karl Marx to wage their war in words, the child must be taken away from its mother, put into a State creche, and the mother sent off to work.

Today the machine can do the work of fifty men thirty years ago. We have roughly a quarter of a million of our people unemployed and in 1989 we banished 49,000 of our finest young men and women to foreign shores, very many of them against their own wishes, especially those who left wife and children at home. Western Europe has 16 million unemployed. Then what sort of crazy world do we live in with such numbers willing and anxious to work condemned to rise each day to no purpose but to exist for yet another few hours when it will be time to retire again. Is it then not madness to foster a policy of pushing mothers who already have more than enough to do out to work. No it is not madness. It was planned that way, for we have a State funded agency, the Employment Equality Agency calling on the Government to encourage mothers to return to the work force, to leave their children who so badly need a mother's love when they return from school to sit in an empty home (any home is empty without a mother) with the T.V. for comfort. No it is not crazy. It is planned that way.

The school was once the place where the teacher took over from the parents, where the child could be left with complete trust. The school is now a war zone, where the mind of the child is the prize. Bigger and bigger schools have been thrust on us by the World Bank to ensure that the herd will rule. The results were plain to see many, many years ago in the U.S. where they have been nemed The Blackboard Jungle and given as the reason Why Johnny Cannot Read. There is no mystery here we are merely following the directives of the vertical chain of command.

It began with the take-over of the Teachers Training Colleges at the beginning of this century and there to implant the teachings of Hegel and Marx. Hegel denied that God is a person apart from the universe He created. He taught that God is in everything that exists, all inclusive, and that everything in the universe is part of God. God would then be reduced to a state of harmless energy, and Man elevated to the position of God. Soulless matter in motion was all there was, and man just another form of matter. This was the temptation of Eve.

John Dewey is regarded as the father of modern education. His idea was not to teach the child to read and write but to train him to fit into the socialist state. He began to fashion a new materialist religion in which humanity was venerated instead of God, the religion of Secular Humanism, now the official religion in the state schools in the U.S.

Dewey's mission was to transform American society from Capitalism to Socialism, and of course, the teaching of evolution, that we are all descended from apes and not from our first parents, Adam and Eve, has been an integral part of the programme. Dewey wrote in My Pedagogic Creed:

I believe therefore that the true centre of correlation on the school subjects is not science, nor literature, nor history, nor geography, but the child's social activities."

quoted in National Education Assn. Journal,
May 1927, P. 134.

In politics when anything happens you can bet it was planned that way was one of F.D.R.'s more famous statements. The take-over of the schools was well planned. What happened in the U.S. yesterday has been planned for us today. In the past ten years we have been told we must have sex education in the schools and that we must have something known as Lifeskills. This particular skill teaches that there is no such thing as right and wrong. What's right for you may be wrong for someone else. If it feels good do it. Ireland's branch of International Planned Parenthood claimed some time ago that it had trained already 2,000 teachers to implement the Lifeskills programme. For more than 1500 years our children have been taught that right is right and wrong is wrong, that the Ten Commandments were given to us to follow in the same way that motorists are commanded to keep the rules of the road. Not any more. Now our children are prepared to fit into the state leading to the world state.

Drink, drugs, pronography and pop music which in many cases is satanic when backtracked, all are part of the war on our children. If our most precious possession, our children, are to be saved they will have to be saved by individuals. In this overwhelmingly Catholic state, for tax purposes, children are regarded as non-existent, for the couple with ten or any number of children get the same tax allowance as the couple with no children.

> *All that is necessary for the triumph of evil is that good men do nothing.*
>
> *Edmund Burke.*

Gary Allen has written:

> *"Youth believes it is rebelling against the Establishment. Yet the Establishment owns and operates the radio and T.V. stations, the mass magazines, and the record companies that have made rock music and its performing artists into a powerful force in American life.*
>
> *Does it not seem strange that the same Establishment which has used the mass media to ridicule and denigrate the anti-Communist movement should open its door to those who think they are the Establishment's enemy.*
>
> *("Who They Are" American Opinion P.69 Oct. 1972)."*

The connection between the music and the purpose of the music was stated by Dr. Timothy Leary, the self-proclaimed King of the Drug L.S.D.:

> *"The person who says rock 'n' roll music encourages kids to take drugs is absolutely right. It's part of our plot..... Drugs are the most efficient way to revolution....."*
>
> *(The Review of The News, Nov. 5, 1969, P.26).*

The family, the basic foundation unit of society is under attack every hour and minute of the day. Hour after hour after hour after hour the television keeps pounding away, glamourising adultery, doing everything in its power to break up the family. It's not the bad guys who are shown to be committing adultery. It is the supposed good guys and it is done with subtlety. Bit by bit the Christian faith of our young people is being eroded and being replaced by the false teachings of secular humanism. When the religion of a people changes so will its laws which will inevitably reflect that change. Here as yet we are protected by our Constitution, but that is under attack as is the Constitution of the U.S. No country will have a Constitution to protect its people when the One Worlders realise their plan for control. There will only be their Constitution for their World State.

CHAPTER 5

The Left and The Right

Politics is a game in the pursuit of power. In all democracies there are two separate organisations playing the game. There is a visible one, whose members hold office as members of a government, and an invisible one, composed of individuals who control the visible, and in whom is vested the real power, that of money, which makes or unmakes its tools.

The visible organisation is divided into the Left and the Right. There are many splinter groups following one or other of these two, but, no matter which of these two groups gains power for a time, the self same line is followed, that of more and more power for Government and less and less for the people who elected it. Ever increasing numbers of people must continually be made dependent on Government.

Whether in or out of Government the motive power lies in the Left. The Right is merely its foil. The aim is to beggar more and more of our hard working people through penal taxation so that there is little difference between the income of the hard working wage earner and the dole drawer.

This is all worked out by the invisible power brokers, who, being nationally irresponsible cannot be called to account for the acts of the governments they control. This is the inherent weakness of any government, the apotheosis of which is the control of both parties in the state, the Left and the Right, radical and conservative, by the same forces. Only the puppets change, while those controlling the machine continue unhindered. Voters who wonder why their efforts have failed, wonder in vain. As the dupes of a controlled publicity their privilege of the vote is a farce. Now if all this is possible at the national level why should it not be so at the international level.

Just as the Pope has a vertical chain of command in the Church (nowadays mostly unheeded) there is a vertical chain of command emanating from the apex of the combination of secret societies that run our secular world, arranged in concentric circles, any operator only knowing his immediate instructor or commander. Daily and hourly the chain of command leads towards total control of the whole human race in a world government. If one cares to compare it to cancer, it is cancer of the whole international body politic, a mad wild growth that will surely be ended by divine intervention as was the Tower of Babel.

CHAPTER 6

The U.S.A.

It is popularly believed that the U.S.A. is a conservative country, the last bastion of free enterprise and freedom. It is also popularly believed that there is deadly enmity between the U.S. and the socialist countries, in particular, the U.S.S.R. And, if there is not some deadly enmity somewhere, why the awful build up of arms, something the world has never known before now.

At this point it is necessary to emphasise that there is a wide gulf between what the outside world understands as the U.S. and the American people as a whole. The American people are about the most naive, uninformed, generous people in the whole world. Alas, the American people have no power. Like Gulliver they are tied down, if not by little men, then by really evil men. For more than two generations the U.S. has been a conquered nation and its people enslaved, as yet not totally, but that is coming. That vast nation is ruled mostly by people of foreign origin and by some natives who are traitors.

America began its march towards slavery with the passing of two laws, the Federal Reserve and the Income Tax Act. Those responsible for the passing of both, the super rich, had already their plans made to protect their riches from the taxman, by the establishment of their so-called Charitable Foundations, whereby their vast wealth would be siphoned into 'Charities' of which they themselves would have complete control. And the main use to which such vast wealth has been put, over the years, was admitted by the head of the Ford Foundation to the Congressional Committee investigating the use of its funds so as bring about a merger of the U.S. and the U.S.S.R.

The U.S. entered two world wars though their people were totally against their entry. Had the U.S. not entered the first World War it would have ended in stalemate and would not have led so soon to the second World War. The first World War could be said to have been fought so that Communism would get a foothold in Russia, and to ensure that it succeeded, American troops were held in Russia until this was certain. And were it not for Wall Street money and that of some European Banks there never would have been a Bolshevik Revolution. This is now fully documented from Government sources in Professor Anthony Sutton's trilogy, **Wall Street and the Bolshevik Revolution**. That it was Wall Street money that set up Hitler with the intention of bringing about the second World War, Professor Sutton has documented in his book **Wall Street and The Rise of Hitler**. That all the technology, the know how, much of the raw material and most of the funds to build the industrial and military machine with which the U.S.S.R. now threatens the free world came from the U.S. cannot now be questioned. That menacing military machine could well be stamped: "Made in the U.S.".

That World War II was fought to extend the Communist empire into Eastern Europe and the Far East is now plain to see. And that extension of the Communist Empire could be said to have been achieved by the action of one man, President F.D. Roosevelt, no doubt on orders from his superiors, from the Vertical Chain of command that today rules the world.

At Yalta three men sat around a table and proceeded to carve up the world, to toss, not millions of people, or tens of millions, but hundreds of millions of human beings around as if they were ants. And who at Yalta possessed the power to make such diabolical decisions, none other than Franklin Delano Roosevelt. At the table Stalin was a beggar, his Forces for two years having its wages paid by the American taxpayer

18

to the tune of nineteen billion dollars. Of course, the said taxpayer didn't know. And yet this beggar Stalin had the war prolonged in Europe by a year and in the Far East by five months so that in Europe his Armies could get to Berlin, and in the Far East, for being five days nominally at war with Japan, he could claim all the spoils for which a quarter of a million Americans lost their lives and millions of others suffered injuries, not to mention the colossal civilian suffering. And that led to the Korean and Vietnam fiascoes.

When the Korean war was about to be ended in a matter of weeks by General McArthur what was to be done with this troublesome General but sack him. There was no other way, and when General Chiang offered to invade the mainland when the Chinese Army had crossed the Yalu River, the U.S. Seventh Fleet was ordered into the Formosa Straits to prevent anything of the kind happening. And Chiang would never have had to flee to Formosa, if General Marshall had not been able to boast that with a stroke of the pen he had disarmed Chiang. "As Chief of Staff "he said" I armed 39 divisions for Chiang, and with a stroke of the pen I disarmed them." Owen Lattimore, spokesman for the establishment, let the cat out of the bag when he said: "The idea was to let Korea fall without making it look as if we pushed it."

It used to be said that in war there is no substitute for victory. Not so today. Today we have the spectacle of what is called no-win wars, and they began in Korea and Vietnam, war had to go on and on, just for the fun of it, and until eventually the Communists could claim all the spoils.

Cuba

Lenin had a plan: First take Eastern Europe, then the Far East, lastly surround that last bastion of Capitalism, the United States, with Communist States, corrupt it from within with drink, drugs and pornography, and it will then fall like rotten fruit into our lap. See the pattern emerging. Now we come to the surrounding of the U.S. with Communist States. How did Castro get control of Cuba! Just as Chiang was disarmed with a stroke of the pen, so was Battista in Cuba, while the U.S. gave the blind eye to the arming of Castro by the U.S.S.R.

After the Castro take-over a group of Cubans who had fled to the U.S. prepared to invade the island to take control out of Castro's hands. From the beginning the venture was set up to fail.

The invasion force of anti-communist forces was prepared in the U.S. One of the early signs that the invasion was planned to fail was the appearance of an article in the New York Times on January 10, 1961, about three months prior to the invasion, with the head-line: "U.S. Helps Train Anti-Castro Force at Secret Air-Ground Base." The article included a map showing the location of the training base. So all Castro had to do to know about the invasion that was to come was to read the New York Times. Its correspondent Herbert Mathews had been repeatedly telling the American people that Castro was not a Communist, but an agrarian reformer, the George Washington of Cuba. The invading forces landed on April, 16, 1961, and were soon in charge of 800 square miles, when suddenly Castro's Air Force took control over the invasion area. The invasion was doomed. Present Kennedy had promised air cover and at the last minute cancelled it. He appeared to be under higher orders. If he hadn't promised air cover the invasion would never have taken place.

The missile crisis was next staged for ulterior motives, as a result of which President Kennedy and the American Government gave assurances to the Russian and Cuban Governments that they would intervene in any invasion of Cuba from anywhere by Anti-Castro forces. Henceforth the U.S. would see that Castro remained in power.

It was later revealed that President Kennedy, as part of the agreement for the Russians to remove the alleged missiles, agreed to remove actual missiles from American bases in Turkey and Italy.

Anti-Castro Cubans, unaware of this agreement between the Russians and the Americans, were purchasing weapons and ships in the United States at the time, and were preparing for a counter-revolution in Cuba. As they moved towards the Cuban shore, they were stopped by the U.S. Coastguard and their ships and weapons were taken away. Uncle Sam was now protecting Fidel.

One who felt that the American government actually created the Castro Movement and later imposed it on the Cuban people was President John F. Kennedy. According to The New York Times of December 11, 1963, President Kennedy gave an interview in which he was quoted as saying: "I think we have spawned, constructed, entirely fabricated without knowing it, the Castro Movement." (Mario Lazo, Dagger in the Heart, American Policy Failures in Cuba, P.94). Soon Herbert Mathews was rewarded for his efforts in bringing Castro to power by being elevated to the Editorial Board of the New York Times.

And President Kennedy, who had begun to wake up, and figure it all out, was dead about three weeks before the Times carried the interview.

Nicaragua

The pattern was repeated in Nicaragua, handed over to the Communists by Jimmy Carter in the name of Civil Rights. Before he was assassinated Somoza had time to tell how it happened published under the title **Somoza Speaks**. As in Korea the idea was that Nicaragua should fall without making it look as if America pushed it.

In the fifties many Americans began to wake up and to try

21

and warn fellow Americans of what was happening. One was Bishop Fulton Sheen who as a T.V. personality began to out-star the film stars. At the height of his popularity when the whole nation seemed to hang on his every word, he suddenly disappeared from the living room, never again to be seen on T.V. Alighting from a plane one day he was met by a reporter who said: "Why do we never see you on T.V. any more?" the Bishop replied: "I've got the money, I've got the sponsors, but the networks won't allow me to speak."

Whitakker Chambers author of the book **"Witness"** who helped convict Soviet Agent, Alger Hiss, describes in his book how the whole weight of the media descended upon him, painting him as a villain, and Hiss as a hero. Chambers in **"Witness"**said the U.S. was divided in three ways: the workers voted for the Democrats, the business people belonged to the Republican party but the Communist party belonged to the super rich. Not surprisingly Eleaner Roosevelt was one of the more outspoken defenders of Hiss. The propaganda was too much for Chambers. It sent him to an early grave.

At the end of World War II the U.S. was a military and economic giant the like of which the world had never before known, and it had the atom bomb. It could have taken on the whole world and beaten it to the ground, even without the bomb, in weeks. In contrast the U.S.S.R. was in a shambles, the wages of its Armed Forces paid for the years 1945 and 1946 by the American taxpayer to the tune of nineteen billion dollars. This information was, of course, carefully kept from the said taxpayer. How then could it come about that in a few short years this military and economic giant quakes before the military might of the country that had been in a shambles in 1945. It may seem to be a mystery, but it is no mystery at all to anyone who knows who runs America. Professor Anthony Sutton throws much light on the supposed mystery in his book **"The**

Best Enemy that Money Can Buy". With no enemy in sight for the military and economic giant, one had to be created, so that the arms race could go on and on. This would give the whole human race something to worry about, with the bomb being psychologically dropped on it every day. In pursuit of Hegel's dialectic a new Marxist Power had to be created. The U.S. possessed the technology. It could order the creation of money with pen and ink and so it set the people of the U.S., to work to build this other Super Power, the U.S.S.R. The working man thought it was great to have work. He didn't ask where his technology was ending up so long as he had work, as the farmer didn't ask where much of his wheat was ending up so long as he had a market, and the taxpayer didn't ask why he was paying taxes to build up this other Super Power.

If the U.S. was serious about fighting Communism would it allow a school for training Communists in Psycholpolitics to operate unhindered by anyone at 1131 Wells Street, Milwaukee, Wisconsin as reported by Kenneth Goff in the Chapter on Psychopolitics. In Rakovsky's words money is power, the only power. Put that power into the hands of a few men and nothing is too bizarre to happen. No country has ever fallen into the hands of the communists without the direct, overt and deliberate action of the United States.

In the newsletter Health Freedom News, Douglas Centre, 2470 Windy Hill Road, Suite 440, Atlanta, GA. William Campbell Douglas, M.D. writes

> *"Communists are in the process of conducting germ warfare from Fort Detrick, Maryland, against the free world, especially the United States, even using foreign Communist agents within the United States Army's germ warfare unit euphamistically called the Army Infectious Disease unit. Carlton Gajdusek, an NIH bigshot at Detrick admits it: 'In*

23

the facility I have a building where more good and loyal Communist Scientists from the U.S.S.R. and Mainland China work, with full passkeys to all the laboratories, than there are American; even the Army's infectious disease unit is loaded with foreign workers not always friendly national.'"

The author claims the AIDS virus was created by the World Health Authority in this laboratory. He goes on,

"It was a cold-blooded successful attempt to create a killer virus which was then used in a successful experiment in Africa. . . . . .

This viral and genetic death bomb, AIDS, was finally produced in 1974. It was given to monkeys and they died of pneumocystis which is typical AIDS. . . . . .What happened in 1978 and beyond to cause AIDS to burst upon the scene? It was the introduction of the hepatitis B vaccine which exhibits the exact epidemology of AIDS. . . . .

A Doctor W. Schmugner, born in Poland and educated in Russia, came to this country in 1969. Schmugner's immigration to the U.S. was probably the most fateful immigration in our history. He, by unexplained process, became head of the New York City blood bank. (How does a Russian trained doctor become head of one of the largest blood banks in the world? Doesn't that strike you as peculiar?)

He set up the rules for the hepatitis vaccine studies. Only males between the ages of 20 and 40, who were not monogamous, would be allowed to participate in this study. . . . . Schmugner is now dead and his diabolical secret went with him. . . . . where is the data on the hepatitis vaccine studies?

24

FDA? CDC? No, the U.S. Department of Justice has it buried where you will never see it."

. . . . .The situation is extremely desperate and the medical profession is too frightened and cowed (as usual) to take any action. Dr. Strecker (the California Doctor who made the discovery) attempted to mobilise the doctors through some of the most respected medical journals in the world. The prestigious Annals of Internal Medicine said that his material 'appears to be entirely concerned with matters of virology' and so try some other publication. In his letter to The Annals Strecker said: "If correct human experimental procedures had been followed we would not find half of the world stumbling off on the wrong path to the cure for AIDS with the other half of the world covering up the origination of the damned disease. It appears to me that your Annals of Internal Medicine is participating in the greatest fraud ever perpetrated.'

Strecker submitted his sensational and mind-boggling letter with all of the proper documentation to the British Journal, Lancet. Their reply: "Thank you for that interesting letter on AIDS. I am sorry to have to report that we will not be able to publish it. We have no criticism but their letter section was 'overcrowded with submissions.'"

CHAPTER 7

The New Age

"Harvard's motto is 'Veritas'. Many of you have already found out and others will find out in the course of their lives that truth eludes us as soon as our concentration begins to flag, all the while leaving the illusion that we are continuing to pursue it. This is the source of much discord. Also, truth seldom is sweet; it is almost invariably bitter.
Solzhenitsyn at Harvard, June 1978

Much is heard today about the New Age Movement. It received its modern start in 1875 with the founding of the Theosophical Society by Helena Blavatsky. Its basic teaching is that all world religions have "common truths" that transcend political differences. Strongly propounding the theory of evolution, the Society also believes in the existence of "Masters". Madame Blavatsky worked in "telepathic communications" serving as a fulcrum for the 'Masters" until her death in 1891. She was followed by Annie Besant. From Annie Besant the leading role was passed to Alice Anne Bailey, a former Christian teacher and wife of an Episcopal rector. Following an unhappy marriage Alice moved to California where she came in contact with Theosophists who encouraged her to join their ranks. She later married Foster Bailey. Alice wrote nearly two dozen books laying out the specific instructions for disciples of the Masters in the latter part of the 20th century - our present time. Like Helena Blavatsky Alice showed tenacious hatred for orthodox Christianity and fierce loyalty to the cause of occultism and Eastern mysticism. In her writings she taught the divinity of man and reincarnation as well as attacking God's work. As part of her work she organised the Arcane School, the New Group of World Servers, Triangles, World Goodwill and assisted with a host of other foundational activities to help build the New Age. Lucifer Publishing Company was established in 1922, the name being changed the following year to Lucis.

Mrs Bailey concentrated on giving disciples directions for networking and infiltration. The Society was to remain in low profile until 1975 when the hitherto secret teachings about the New Age Christ and its hierarchy could be publicly disseminated.

Alice's teachings gave step by step instructions for the institution of the New World Order - plans for religious war, forced redistribution of the world's resources, Luciferic initiations, mass planetary initiations, theology for the New World Religion, disarmament and the elimination or scaling away of obstinate religious orthodoxies.

To prepare for this New Age it is argued that men and women must first alter conventional ways of thinking. They must enter an altered state of consciousness through the use of such types of psychological techniques as meditation, hypnosis, chanting, bio-feedback, prolonged isolation and the intervention of "Spirit Guides". While in this altered state leaders of the groups are able to implant new ideas and alter their thinking processes, a form of mind control.

It is argued that mankind is at the threshold of "a great evolutionary leap of consciousness" to new beliefs about many things, and that there is an energy or force in the universe that will lead to a happy, peaceful, united new world.

The New York Times of September 29, 1986, in a cover story provides some insights into the New Age Movement. It rejects the idea of a single Omnipotent God who has revealed His will to man. New Agers follow the view of many Eastern Religions that there is unity in the universe of which all things, including God and man are equal parts. According to this view man himself is a deity who can "create his own reality." Sociologists say this view is a foundation of the "Human Potential" training programmes. This is really the temptation of Eve all over again. God is in His creation, not separate from it. We are all part of it. We are all gods evolving towards an omega point. Eve only had to eat the apple. All we have to do is allow the implantation of their ideas in our minds.

The New Age has four goals:

1.   To usher in a new World Order,
2.   To launch a new World Religion,
3.   To bring forth a New Age Christ,
4.   To pay universal honour and homage to Lucifer (their Light Bearer).

Winston: *What will this New Order or New Age be like?*
O'Brien: *The jackboot forever on the human face.*
from 1984 by George Orwell

CHAPTER 8

The Catholic Church and Freemasonry

As already pointed out the Illuminati infiltrated and took command of the Masonic Lodges in France. It was due to this take-over that the French Revolution was brought on with such haste. Napoleon became a stumbling block and caused a set-back in their plans, but having successfully defeated him in 1815, they issued what became known as Permanent Instructions, as a guide to the higher initiated who were chosen to command the whole Masonic movement, especially in Italy. The following excerpts comprise but a small part of the full instructions as quoted in Lady Queenborough's Occult Theocrasy, P.430.

> *Our final aim is that of Voltaire and of the French Revolution - the complete annihilation of Catholicism, and ultimately of Christianity. Were Christianity to survive, even upon the ruins of Rome, it would, a little later on, revive and live....*

> *....The Papacy has been for seventeen hundred years interwoven with the history of Italy....*

> *The Pope, whoever he may be, will never enter into a secret society. It then becomes the duty of the Secret Society to make the first advance to the Church and to the Pope, with the object of conquering both. The work for which we gird ourselves up, is not the work of a day, nor of a month nor of a year. It may last for many years, perhaps for a century; in our ranks the soldier dies, but the war is continued....*

Catholics! What must we consider Freemasonry, when freemasons themselves pronounce it an apostasy from Catholicity, and foresee that a power fully acquainted with them and their machinations would, as a consequence, seek to crush them.

That which we seek, that which we await, as the Jews await a Messiah, is a Pope according to our wants. An Alexander VI would not suit us, for he never erred in religious doctrine; a Pope Borgia would not suit us, for he was excommunicated by all the thinking philosophers and unbelievers for the vigour with which he defended the Church. We require a Pope for ourselves, if such a Pope were possible. With such a one we should march more securely to the storming of the Church than with all the little books of our French and English brothers.

And why? Because it were useless to seek with these alone to split the rock upon which God has built His Church. We should not want the vinegar of Hannibal, nor gunpowder, nor even our arms, if we had but the little finger of the successor of Peter engaged in the plot; that little finger would avail us more for our crusade than all the Urbans II and St. Bernards for the crusade of Christianity. We trust that we may yet attain this supreme object of our efforts....

That the Church has been infiltrated in order to destroy it can now be seen plainly. Confrontation would have been useless. It had to be infiltration. The year before the present Holy Father became Pope, in an address to the Eucharistic Congress in the United States, he stated that the Catholic Church is now in the final confrontation with evil, that the

Church which the devil will set up, externally may look like the one true Church, the Catholic Church, but it will be the Church of the Anti-Christ.

Some self-professed ex-Communists have been telling us about this infiltration. Dr. Bella Dodd, who was head of the Communist Party in New York during and following World War II and who later left the Party when she came to realise that there was a higher Conspiracy than the Communist one, said that she personally had advised almost one thousand of the finest young men she knew in the Party to enter Catholic seminaries to become priests and Bishops. Another ex-Communist, Mr. Manning Johnson, after he left the Communist Worker's Party of the U.S., stated in evidence before a Congressional Committee examining un-American activities in the year 1953, that in 1936 the Party had received orders from Moscow that all members were to go back into their ancestral Churches, and there to seek positions of control of the grass roots, President, Chairperson, Secretary, etc. Radicals of every hue were told to enter seminaries with the intention of becoming Priests. In this, Mr. Johnson stated, the party was successful beyond its most optimistic expectations. He further stated that the Party had two goals in infiltrating the Church. One was to neutralise its anti-Communist character. Encyclical after encyclical had been written by successive Popes condemning Communism in the strongest terms, Pope Pius XI in his Encyclical on Communism stating that "Communism is intrinsically evil, and no one who would save civilisation may collaborate with it in any undertaking whatever." The second goal of the Party was to divert clerical thinking and teaching away from the spiritual to the social and political. Henceforth the subject of sin was to be taboo. The Ten Commandments and the Seven Sacraments were not to be mentioned, and of course the idea of Hell was to be laughed to scorn. Mr. Johnson stated the Party discovered from experience that all it needed was one per cent of any organisation in order to control it. Why, because they acted as one, and the others acted individually. He said too you could get fellow travellers, liberals, what Lenin called useful idiots. If they could get nine per cent useful idiots to work with the one per cent, they could effectively control any Church or any organisation that they infiltrated. The aim was to control the lines of power in the Chancery offices to prevent a Bishop hearing anything not approved by the Party.

The first target was the schools. In 1969, these dissenters, as they are known, were boasting that they controlled the Parochial Schools and all Catechetical instruction.

How well the Party did its work in the United States can now be judged by just a few results - 125,000 nuns have left religious life as well as 50,000 priests. The average age of nuns today is 64 years and priests 58 years old. In the Boston Diocese in 1958, 72 priests were ordained. In 1989 just three prepared for ordination. The Bishop of Detroit Diocese regrets that he must close 43 churches. This is a small example of what is happening in one country in a few short years.

In Britain things are not noticeably different. There, 46 per cent of the time given to Christian Doctrine, is devoted to the study of all other religions, both Christian and non-Christian, but not to point out any defects or heresies in those religions.

Up to the time of the Reformation the Church looked after the poor, the sick, the elderly. There was no need of Government aid in any of these services. Christianity had to be uprooted in order that Government everywhere could become Big Brother and turn all three into Big Business for itself. It was then the word pauper entered the English language.

The Rome-Moscow Agreement

At the Second Vatican Council which commenced in 1962 there were a number of non-Catholic observers. Among the churches represented was the Russian Orthodox Church, represented by Monsgr. Nikodim. Prior to attending the Council the Russian Orthodox Church insisted on an Agreement being formally signed between itself and the Vatican in which the Vatican was required to give an undertaking that at the Council there would be no criticism of, or reference to Communism. This was given a low profile in the Media. The Communist press was the first to disclose the Agreement, and, on this point, it has never been denied or contradicted. 'France Nouvelle', the leading weekly of the Party on Page 15 of the week January 16-22, 1963, had this to say:-

Since the world socialist system shows its superiority indisputably and enjoys the approval of many hundreds of millions of men, the Church can no longer rest content with crude anti-Communism. She has even given an undertaking on the occasion of her dialogue with the Russian Orthodox church, that there would be no direct attack on the Communist regime at the Council.

A few days later, on Page 5 of its February 15 issue, 'La Croix' referred to the Agreement, ending its commentary with the words "Mgr. Nikodim agreed that someone should go to Moscow to convey an invitation provided that a pledge were given as to the non-political attitude of the Council."

The French magazine 'Itineraire' had written in its June, 1964, issue (No. 84, P. 39-40):

"The presence of Soviet Orthodox observers at the first session of the Council was negotiated with Mgr. Nikodim. The negotiations were held at Metz in 1962....

Mgr. Nikodim had sought 'pledges' about which no public information from Catholic sources is available....

The Communists, on their part, publicly assert that the Catholic Church had given an undertaking, on the occasion of her dialogue with the Russian Orthodox Church, that there would be no direct attack on the Communist regime at the Council."

It appears the Agreement was kept to the letter at the Council, for 400 Bishops signed a petition to have the subject of Communism discussed at the Council, but their petition never reached the Agenda. See "The Rhine Flows into the Tiber" by Fr. Wiltgens, an American reporter at the Council.

Nikodim died in the arms of Pope John Paul I. One of the many rumours circulating is that he drank from a glass of wine intended for the Pope.

The Church on earth is the Church militant. But what is the institutional Church militant against today – certainly not its greatest enemy!

CHAPTER 9

Psychopolitics

Psychopolitics is a branch of war-making, unknown, at least to the general public, in the West. As will be shown from quotations from the teaching manual set before students who are chosen to conduct this form of warmaking it is something the public need to fear far more than the most powerful weapons. Bombs can only destroy bodies. Psychopolitics strikes at the very core and soul of man. If the Government of the day in any country, in the so-called free West, will not do anything to protect its people from this deadly menace, the people must protect themselves. They cannot protect themselves against something of which they know nothing, so the first vital necessity is knowledge of what psychopolitics is. Christ himself said: "The truth will set you free."

The following quotations from the teaching manual speak for themselves, further comment is not considered necessary:

> *Although punishment for its own sake may not be entirely without recompense, it is, nevertheless true that the end and goal of all punishment is the indoctrination of the person being punished, with an idea, whether that idea be one of restraint or obedience.*

> *The stupidity and narrowness of nations not blessed with Russian reasoning has caused them to rely upon practices which are, today, too ancient and out-moded for the rapid and heroic pace of our time.; And in view of the tremendous advance of Russian Culture in the field of mental technologies, begun with the glorious work of Pavlov, and carried*

forward so ably by later Russians, it would be strange that an art and science would not evolve totally devoted to the aligning of loyalties and extracting the obedience of individuals and multitudes.... In psychopolitical procedures there is no ethical problem, since it is obvious and evident that Man is always coerced against his will....

Basically, man is an animal. Those who so group and control him must then have in their possession specialised techniques to direct the vagaries and energies of the animal Man....

Psychopolitics is the art and science of asserting and maintaining dominion over the thoughts and loyalties of individuals, officers, bureaus, and masses, and the effecting of the conquest of the enemy nations through "mental healing."

The subject of Psychopolitics breaks down into several categories.......... The next is the anatomy of the stimulus response mechanism of Man. The next is the subject of shock and endurance..... The next is the use of drugs. The next is the use of implantation...... The next is the organisation and use of counter-Psychopolitics..... The next is the creation of slave philosophy in an hostile nation.... To this might be added many categories, such as the nullification of modern weapons by psychopolitical activity....

In nations less enlightened, where the Russian State does not yet have power, it is not as feasible to remove the entire self-willed individual. Psychopolitics makes it possible to remove that part of his personality which, in itself, is making havoc with the group...... Just as in hypnotism any organ can be commanded into greater loyalty and obedience, so can any political group be commanded into greater loyalty and obedience should sufficient force be employed....

In this time of unlimited weapons, and in national antagonisms where atomic war with Capitalistic powers is possible, Psychopolitics must act efficiently as never before.

Any and all programs of Psychopolitics must be increased to aid and abet the activities of other Communist agents throughout the nation in question.

The failure of Psychopolitics might well bring about the atomic bombing of the Motherland.

If Psychopolitics succeeds in its mission throughout the Capitalistic nations of the world, there will never be an atomic war, for Russia will have subjugated all of her enemies.

Communism has already spread across one-sixth of the inhabited world. Marxist Doctrines have already penetrated the remainder. An extension of the Communist social order is everywhere victorious. The spread of Communism has never been by force of battle, but by conquest of the mind. In Psychopolitics we have refined this conquest to its last degree.

The psychopolitical operative must succeed, for his success means a world of Peace. His failure might well mean the destruction of the civilized portions of Earth by atomic power in the hands of Capitalistic madmen.

The end thoroughly justifies the means. The

degradation of populaces is less inhuman than their destruction by atomic fission, for to an animal who lives only once, any life is sweeter than death.

The end of war is the control of a conquered people. If a people can be conquered in the absence of war, the end of war will have been achieved without the destruction of war. A worthy goal.

The psychopolitician has his reward in the nearly unlimited control of populaces, in the uninhibited exercise of passion, and the glory of Communist conquest over the stupidity of the enemies of the People.

The masses must at last come to believe that only excessive taxation of the rich can relieve them of the 'burdensome leisure-class" and can thus be brought to accept such a thing as Income Tax, a Marxist principle, smoothly slid into the Capitalistic framework in 1909, in the United States. This, even though the basic law of the United States forbade it, and even though Communism at that time had been active only a few years in America. Such success as the Income Tax law, had it been followed thoroughly, could have brought the United States and not Russia into the world scene as the first Communist nation.

The Communist agent skilled in economics has as his task the suborning of tax agencies and their personnel to create the maximum disturbance and chaos and the passing of laws adapted to our purposes and to him we must leave this task.

The rich, the skilled in finance, the well informed

in government are particular and individual targets for the psychopolitician. His is the role of taking off the board those individuals who would halt or corrupt Communist economic progress. Thus every rich man, every statesman, every person well informed and capable in government must have brought at his side, as a trusted confidant, a psychopolitical operator.... The normal health and wildness of a rich man's son must be twisted and perverted and assisted by a timely administration of drugs, or violence turned into criminality or insanity. This brings at once some one in "mental healing" into confidential contact with the family and from this point on the very most must be made of that contact.

Communism could best succeed if at the side of every rich or influential man there could be placed a psychopolitical operator.... who could by his advice embroil or upset the economic policies of the country and, when the time comes, to do away forever with the rich or influential man, to administer the proper drug or treatment to bring about his complete demise in an institution as a patient or dead as a suicide.

Planted beside a country's powerful persons the psychopolitical operator can also guide other policies to the betterment of our battle.

The Capitalist does not know the definition of war. He thinks of war as attack with force performed by soldiers and machines. He does not know that a more effective, if somewhat longer war can be fought with bread, or in our case, with drugs and the wisdom of our art. The Capitalist has never won a war in truth. The psychopolitician is having little trouble in winning this one....

Without force and threat there can be no striving. Without pain there can be no desire to escape from pain. Without the threat of punishment there can be no gain....

It is not always necessary to remove the individual.... The technicalities of Psychopolitics are graduated upon the scale which starts somewhat above the removal of the individual himself, upward toward the removal only of those tendencies which bring about his lack of co-operation.

All that it is necessary to do, where disloyalty is encountered, is to align the purposes of the individual towards the goals of Communism, and it will be discovered that a great many circumstances hitherto distasteful in his existence will cease to exist....

The changing of loyalty consists, in its primary step, of the eradication of existing loyalties. This can be done in one of two ways. First, by demonstrating that previously existing loyalties have brought about perilous physical circumstances, such as imprisonment, lack of recognition, duress, or privation, and second, by eradicating the personality itself.... As part of this there is the creation of a state of mind in the individual, by actually placing him under duress, and then furnishing him with false evidence to demonstrate that the target of his previous loyalties is, itself, the cause of the duress...

In moments of expediency, of which there are many, the personality itself can be rearranged by shock, surgery, duress, privation, and in particular, that best of psychopolitical techniques, implantation, with the technologies of neohypnotism. Such duress must have in its first part a defamation of the loyalties, and in its second, the implantation of new loyalties. A good and experienced psychopolitical operator, working under the most favourable circumstances, can, by the use of psychopolitical technologies, alter the loyalties of an individual so deftly that his own companions will not suspect that they have been changed. This however, requires considerably more finesse than is usually necessary to the situation. Mass neo-hypnotism can accomplish more or less the same results when guided by an experienced psychopolitic operator. An end goal in such a procedure would be the alteration of the loyalties of an entire nation in a short period of time by mass neo-hypnotism, a thing which has been effectively accomplished among the less-usable states of Russia.

It is adequately demonstrated that loyalty is entirely lacking in that mythical commodity known as 'spiritual quality'. Loyalty is entirely a thing of dependence, economic or mental, and can be changed by the crudest implementations..... Any man who cannot be persuaded into Communist rationale is, of course, to be regarded as somewhat less than sane, and it is, therefore completely justified to use techniques of insanity upon the non-Communist..... In a case of a very important person, it may be necessary to utilize the more delicate technologies of Psychopolitics so as to place the person himself, and his associates, in ignorance of the operation. In this case a simple implantation is used with a maximum duress and command value. Only the most skilled psychopolitical operator should be employed on such a project, as in this case of the very important person, for a bungling might disclose the tampering with his mental processes..... In securing the loyalty of a very important person one must place at this side a constant pleader who enters a sexual or familial chord into the situation on the side of Communism..... By the use of various drugs, it is, in this modern age, entirely too easy to bring about a state of severe neurosis or insanity in the wife or children, and thus pass them, with full consent of the very important person, and the government in which he exists, or the bureau in which he is operating, into the hands of a psychopolitical operator, who then in his own laboratory, without restraint or fear of investigation or censor, can, with electric shock, surgery, sexual attack, drugs, or other useful means, degrade or entirely alter the personality of a family member, and create in that person a psychopolitical slave subject, who, on command or signal, will perform outrageous actions, thus discrediting the important person, or will demand, on a more delicate level, that certain measures be taken by the important person, which measures are, of course, dictated by the psychopolitical operator.....

When the loyalty of an individual cannot be swerved, and where the opinion, weight, or effectiveness of the individual stands in the way of

Communist goals, it is usually best to occasion a mild neurosis in person by any available means, and then having carefully given him a history of mental imbalance, to see to it that he disposes of himself by suicide, or by bringing about his demise in such a way as to resemble suicide. Psychopolitical operators have handled such situations skillfully tens of thousands of times within and without Russia....

One of the first and foremost missions of the psychopolitician is to make an attack upon Communism and insanity synonymous. It should become the definition of insanity, of the paranoid variety, that "A paranoid believes he is being attacked by Communists." Thus, at once, the support of the individual so attacking Communism, will fall away and wither.

The cleverness of our attack in this field of Psychopolitics is adequate to avoid the understanding of the layman and the usual stupid official, and by operating entirely under the banner of authority with the oft-repeated statement that the principles of psychotherapy are too devious for common understanding, an entire revolution can be effected without the suspicion of a populace until it is an accomplished fact.

As insanity is the maximum mis-alignment, it can be grasped to be the maximum weapon in severance of loyalties to leaders and old social orders. Thus it is of the utmost importance that psychopolitical operatives infiltrate the healing arts of a nation marked for conquest and bring from that quarter continuous pressure against the population and the government until at last the conquest is effected. This is the subject and goal of Psychopolitics itself.....

Space does not permit further quotations. The reader is urged to read the complete Treatise for himself.

The folowing is an address given by Beria to American students at the Marxist Leninist school in Moscow:

An Address by Beria

American students at the Lenin University, I welcome your attendance at these classes on Psychopolitics.

Psychopolitics is an important if less known division of Geopolitics. It is less known because it must necessarily deal with highly educated personnel, the very top strata of "mental healing."

By psychopolitics our chief goals are effectively carried forward. To produce a maximum of CHAOS in the culture of the enemy is our first most important step. Our fruits are grown in chaos, distrust, economic depression and scientific turmoil. At least a very weakened populace can seek peace only in our offered Communist State, at last only Communism can resolve the problems of the masses.

A psychopolitician must work hard to produce the maximum CHAOS in the fields of "mental healing." He must recruit and use all the agencies and facilities of "mental healing." He must labor to increase the personnel and facilities of "mental healing" until at last the entire field of mental science is entirely dominated by Communist principles and desires.

44

To achieve these goals the psychopolitican must crush every "home-grown" variety of mental healing in America. Actual teachings of James Eddy and Pentecostal Bible faith healers amongst your misguided people must be swept aside. They must be discredited, defamed, arrested, stamped upon even by their own government until there is no credit in them and only Communist-oriented "Healing" remains. you must work until every teacher on psychology unknowingly or knowingly teaches only Communist doctrine under the guise of "psychology." You must labor until every doctor and psychiatrist is either a psycho-politician or an unwitting assistant to our aims.

You must labor until we have dominion over the minds and bodies of every important person in your nation. You must achieve such disrepute for the state of insanity and such authority over its pronouncements that not one statesman so labeled could again be given credence by his people. You must work until suicide arising from mental imbalance is common, and calls forth no general investigation or remark.

With the institutions for the insane you have in your country prisons which can hold a million persons and can hold them without civil rights or any hope of freedom. And upon these people can be practised shock and surgery so that never again will they draw a sane breath. You must make these treatments common and accepted. And you must sweep aside any treatment or any group of persons seeking to treat by effective means.

You must dominate as respected men the fields of psychiatry and psychology. You must dominate

45

the hospitals and universities. You must carry forward the myth that only a European doctor is competent in the field of insanity and thus excuse amongst you the high incidence of foreign birth and training. If and when we seize Vienna you shall have then a common ground of meeting and can come and take your instructions as worshippers of Freud along with other psychiatrists.

The following is an account given by Kenneth Goff who published the document on psychopolitics.

From May 2, 1936, to October 10, 1939, I was a dues-paying member of the Communist Party, operating under my own name Kenneth Goff, and also the alias John Keats. In 1939, I voluntarily appeared before the Un-American Activities Committee in Washington, D.C., which was chaired at that time by Martin Dies, and my testimony can be found in Volume 9 of the year's Congressional Report.

During the period that I was a member of the Communist Party, I attended their school which was located at 113 E. Wells Street, Milwaukee, Wisconsin, and operated under the name Eugene Debs Labor School. Here we were trained in all phases of warfare, both psychological and physical, for the destruction of the Capitalistic society and Christian civilization. In one portion of our studies we went thoroughly into the matter of psychopolitics. This was the art of capturing the minds of a nation through brainwashing and fake mental health - the subjecting of whole nations of people to the rule of the Kremlin by the capturing of their minds. We were taught that the degradation of the populace is less inhuman than their destruction by bombs, for to an animal, who lives only once, any life is sweeter than death. The end of a war is the control of a conquered people. If people can be conquered in the absence of war the end of the war will have been achieved without the destruction of war.

During the past few years I have noted with horror the increase of psychopolitical warfare upon the American public. First in the brain-washing of our boys in Korea, and then in the well-financed drive of mental health propaganda by left-wing pressure groups, wherein many of our states have passed Bills which can well be used by the enemies of America to subject to torture and imprisonment those who preach the gospel of our Lord and Saviour Jesus Christ, and who oppose the menace of Communism. A clear example of this can be seen in the Lucille Miller case. In this warfare the Communists have definitely stated: "You must recruit every agency of the nation marked for slaughter into a foaming hatred of religious hearing."

Another example of the warfare that is being waged can be seen in the attempt to establish a mental Siberia in Alaska, which was called for in the Alaskan Mental Health Bill. A careful study of this Bill will make you see at once that the land set aside under the allotment could not be for that small territory, and the Bill within itself establishes such authority that it could be turned into a prison camp, under the guise of mental health, for everyone who raises their voice against Communism and the hidden government operating in our nation.

This book was used in underground schools, and contains the address of Beria to the American students in the Lenin university prior to 1936. The text in the book in general is from the Communist Manual of Instructions of Psychopolitical Warfare, and was used in America for the training of Communist cadre. The only revision in this book is the summary, which was added by the Communists after the atomic bomb was dropped in Japan. In its contents you can see the diabolical plot of the enemies of Christ and America, as they seek to conquer our nation by subjecting the minds of our people to their will by various sinister means.

This manual of the Communist Party should be in the hands of every loyal American, that they may be alerted to the fact that it is not always by armies and guns that a nation is conquered.

Kenneth Goff

CHAPTER **10**

Rakovsky

*Freedom is the freedom to say two plus two
make four.*

p. 200, Nineteen Eighty-Four , George Orwell

Christian G. Rakovsky, a founder member of Communism in the U.S.S.R. and who later became the Soviet Ambassador to Paris, became a victim of Stalin's purges and the show-trials of 1938. He was tried with Bukharin, Rykoff, Yogoda, Dr. Levin and others.

While in the Lubianka, Rakovsky made it clear, having in mind the sparing of his life, that he could give information about matters of very special interest to Stalin. Stalin was interested enough to order his foreign agent, Gavriil G. Kusmin, known as Gabriel, to question Rakovsky.

The interview that followed, from which we quote excerpts, has been taken from a book published in Spain called "La Lucha Por El Poder Mundial," and translated into English by George Knupffer who himself wrote "The Struggle for World Power", an expose of the Higher Conspiracy that controls both the Left and the Right.

Now more than 60 years later the world media keeps up the illusion that Hitler was solely responsible for starting World War II. While plans were in motion to bring about the war one way or another the pages that follow show, without the shadow of a doubt, that the war was triggered off by the proposals set out by Rakovsky and accepted by Stalin. In return for the Plan, Rakovsky managed to save his life, rather as we shall see, Stalin was ordered to spare it.

The interview was witnessed by one Dr. Landowsky, a Russianised Pole, who lived in Moscow, and who was the son of a Colonel in the Russian Imperial Army shot by Bolsheviks during the 1917 Revolution. Against his wishes Dr. Landowsky was forced to witness many torture sessions. This gave him an abhorrence of Communism. He was now ordered to build up Rakovsky's health for the questioning and then to be present at it. As the questioning took place in French, Dr. Landowsky was asked to translate it into Russian. This he did, making an extra copy, which he reserved for posterity. The original document will be found in the Russian archives. How many people anywhere know what lies hidden away in Government Archives.

The exact timing of the questioning is important. It took place from Midnight on January 25, 1938 to 6 a.m. on January 26th. Here it is important to note that Moscow time is three hours ahead of Western European time. As reported in the daily press all over Western Europe and even in the New York Times on January 26, 1938, a strange bright light lit up the sky all across Europe for three hours from 6.30 p.m. to 9.30 p.m. the evening before. This would have been between 9.30 p.m. and 12.30 a.m. Moscow time, at which time the serious questioning of Rakovsky began i.e. 12.30a.m..

When the bright light shone in the sky Sr. Lucia in her Convent in Spain let it be known that this was the sign given by God that the War was about to begin and foretold by Our Lady on 13th July, 1917, that World War II would be preceded by a bright unknown light in the sky all across Europe.

Readers seriously interested in knowing what goes on behind the scenes, referred to by D'Israeli in Coningsby, (and he ought to have known), would be advised to read the questioning in full in a booklet called "Red Symphony" by J. Landowsky and published by The Plain Speaker Publishing Co., 43 Bath Road, London W6.

The Interview

The questioning of the Accused Christian G. Rakovsky by Gavriil Gavriilovitch Kus'min on 26 January 1938:

G. *And you are Hitler's spies?*

R. *Yes.*

G. *No, Rakovsky, no. Tell the real truth, but not the court proceedings one.*

R. *We agreed that at the present moment the opposition cannot be interested in defeatism and the fall of Stalin..... However there is in existence a possible aggressor. There he is the great nihilist Hitler, who is aiming, with his terrible weapon of the Wehrmacht, at the whole horizon. Whether we want it or not, but he will use it against the U.S.S.R? Let us agree that for us this is the decisive unknown factor. Do you consider that the problem has been correctly stated?*

G. *It has been well put. But I can say that for me there is no unknown factor. I consider the attack of Hitler on the U.S.S.R. to be inevitable.*

R. *Why?*

G. *Very simple; because he who controls it is inclined towards attack. Hitler is only the condottiere of international Capitalism.*

R. *You forget something very important. The re-armament of Hitler and the assistance he received at the present time from the Versailles nations (take good note of this) – were received by him during a special period, when we could still have become the heirs of Stalin in the case of his defeat, when the opposition still existed... Do you consider this fact to be a matter of chance or only a coincidence in time?*

G. *..... The destruction of Communism and expansion*

in the East — these are dogmas from the book "Mein Kampf", that Talmud of National-Socialism..... The Hitlerist attack on the U.S.S.R. is, in addition, a dialectical necessity; it is the same as the inevitable struggle of the classes in the international plane. At the side of Hitler, inevitably, there will stand the whole global Capitalism.

R.   *And so, believe me, that in the light of your scholastic dialectics I have formed a very negative opinion about the political culture of Stalinism.* **I listen to your words as Einstein could listen to a schoolboy talking about physics in four dimensions. I see that you are only acquainted with elementary Marxism, i.e. the demagogic, popular one.**

..... In this same elementary Marxism, which is taught even in your Stalinist University, you can find the statement which contradicts the whole of your thesis about the inevitability of the Hitlerist attack on the U.S.S.R.

..... Do you not see that I had reasons for qualifying your Marxist culture as being doubtful? Your argument and reactions are the same as any rank and file activist.

G.   *And they are wrong?*

R.   **Yes, they are correct for a small administrator, for a bureaucrat and for the mass. They suit the average fighter. They must believe this and repeat everything as it has been written.** *Listen to me by way of the completely confidential. With Marxism you get the same results as with the ancient esoteric religions. Their adherents had to know only that which was the most elementary and crude, insofar as by this one provoked their faith,* *i.e. that which is absolutely essential, both in religion and in the work of revolution.*

G. *Do you not now want to open up to me the mystical Marxism, something like yet another freemasonry?*

R. *No, no esoterics.... Marxism, before being a philosophical, economic and political system, is a conspiracy for the revolution.*

*..... it follows that philosophy, economics and politics are true only insofar as they lead to revolution..... "Communism" he says (Marx) "must win because Capital will give it that victory, though its enemy." Such is the magisterial thesis of Marx. Can there be a greater irony? And then, in order that he should be believed, **it was enough for him to depersonalise Capitalism and Communism**.....*

G. *Therefore you deny the existence of the dialectical process of contradictions in Capitalism, which lead to the final triumph of Communism?*

R. *You can be sure that if Marx believed that Communism will achieve victory only thanks to the contradictions in Capitalism, then he would not have once, never, mentioned the contradictions on the thousands of pages of this scientific revolutionary work..... The revolutionary and conspirator will never disclose to his opponent the secret of his triumph... He would never give the information; **he would give him disinformation** which you use in counter-conspiracy.....*

..... Marx deceives for tactical reasons about the origin of the contradictions in Capitalism, but not about their obvious reality, Marx knew how they were created, how they became more acute and how things went towards general anarchy in Capitalistic production, which came before the triumph

of the Communist revolution..... **He knew it would happen because he knew those who created the contradictions.**

G.   *It is a very strange revelation and piece of news, this assertion and exposal of the circumstance that which leads Capitalism to its "suicide".... is not the essence and inborn law of Capitalism.*

R.   **Have you not noticed how in Marx words contradict deeds?** *He declares the necessity and inevitability of Capitalist contradictions, proving the existence of surplus value and accumulation, i.e. he proves that which really exists. He nimbly invests the proposition that to a greater concentration of the means of production corresponds a greater mass of the proletariat, a greater force for the building of Communism, is that not so, Now go on: at the same time as this assertion he founds the International. Yet the International is, in the work of the daily struggle of the classes, a "reformist," i.e. an organisation, whose purpose is the limitation of the surplus value and, where possible, its elimination. For this reason, objectively, the International is a counter-revolutionary organisation and anti-Communist, in accordance with Marx's theory.*

G.   *Now we get that Marx is a counter-revolutionary and an anti-Communist.*

R.   *..... One comes to such absurd conclusions, while they seem to be obvious, when one forgets that* **words and facts in Marxism are subject to the strict rules of the higher science: the rules of conspiracy and revolution.**

..... A strike is already an attempt at revolutionary

mobilisation. Independently of whether it wins or not its economic effect is anarchical.....

Thus to the contradictions in the bourgeois system are added contradictions within the proletariat: this is the double weapon of the revolution, and it - which is obvious - does not arise in itself: **there exists an organisation, chiefs, discipline,** *and above that there exists stupidity.* **Don't you suspect that the much-mentioned contradictions of Capitalism, and in particular the financial ones, are also organised by someone?....** *By way of basis for these deductions I shall remind you that in its economic struggle the Proletarian International coincides with the Financial International, since both produce inflation, and* **wherever there is coincidence there, one should assume, is also agreement.** *Those are his own words.*

G.   *I suspect here such an enormous absurdity, or the intention of spinning a new paradox, that I do not want to imagine this. It looks as if you want to hint at the existence of something like a Capitalist second Communist International, of course an enemy one.*

R.   *Exactly so. When I spoke of the Financial International, I thought of it as of a Comintern, but having admitted the existence of the "Comintern," I would not say that they are enemies...........*

I shall remind you of some very curious things. Notice with what penetration Marx comes to conclusions given the then existence of early British industry; how he analyses it and criticises; what a repulsive picture he gives of the manufacturer, *fat-bellied with a cigar in his mouth, as described by Marx, with self-satisfaction and anger throwing the wife and daughter of the worker onto the street. Is that not so? At the same time remember the moderation of Marx and his bourgeois orthodoxy when studying the question of money. In the problem of money there do not appear with him his famous contradictions. Finances do not exist for him as a thing of importance in itself; trade and the circulation of moneys are the result of the cursed system of Capitalistic production, which subjects them to itself and fully determines them; in the question of money Marx is a reactionary; to ones immense surprise bear in mind the "five-pointed star" like the Soviet one, which shines all over Europe, the star composed of the five Rothschild brothers with their banks, who possess colossal accumulations of wealth, the greatest ever known.... And so this fact, so colossal that it misled the imagination of the people of that epoch, **passes unnoticed by Marx. Something strange.... Is that not so?** It is possible that from this strange blindness of Marx there arises a phenomenon which is common to all future revolution. It is this: **we can all confirm that when the masses take possession of a city or a country, then they always seem struck by a sort of superstitions fear of the banks and bankers.** One had killed kings, generals, bishops, policemen, priests and other representatives of the hated privileged classes; one robbed and burnt palaces, churches and even centres of science, but though the revolutions were economic-social, the lives of the bankers were re-*

*spected, and as a result **the magnificent buildings of the banks remained untouched....** According to my information, before I had been arrested, this continues even now....*

G. *Where?*

R. *In Spain.. Don't you know it? As you ask me, so tell me now. Do you not find all this very strange? Think, the police... I do not know, have you paid attention to the strange similarity which exists between the Financial International and the Proletarian International. I would say that one is the other side of the other, and the back side of the proletarian one as being more modern than the financial.*

G. *Where do you see similarity in things so opposed?*

R. *Objectively they are identical.... **Now we can already guess the reasons why Marx concealed the financial contributions, which could not have remained hidden from his penetrating gaze, if finances had not had an ally,** the influence of which - objectively revolutionary - was already then extraordinarily important.*

G. *An unconscious coincidence, but not an alliance which presupposes intelligence, will and agreement....*

R. *.... let us see what sort of people personally are at work there. The international essence of money is well known. From this fact emerges that the organisation which owns them and accumulates them is a cosmopolitan organisation. Finances in their apogee as an aim in themselves, the financial International - **deny and do not recognise anything national, they do not recognise the State;***

and therefore it is anarchical and would be abso-
lutely anarchical if it - the denier of any national
*State - were not itself, by necessity, **a State in its***
own basic essence. The State as such is only
***power.** And money is exclusively power.*

This communistic super-state, which we are creat-
ing already during a whole century, and the scheme
of which is the International of Marx: Analyse it,
and you will see its essence, the scheme of the
International and its prototype of the U.S.S.R. -
that is also pure power. The basic similarity
between the two creations is absolute. It is some-
thing fatalistic, inevitable, since the personalities
*of the authors of both were identical. **The finan-***
cier is just as international as the Communist.
Both, with the help of differing pretext and differ-
ing means, struggle with the national bourgeois
State and deny it, Marxism in order to change it
into a Communist State; from this comes that the
Marxist must be an internationalist; the financier
denies the bourgeois national state and his denial
ends in itself; in fact he does not manifest himself
as an internationalist, but as a cosmopolitan anar-
chist.....

Money is power. Money is today the centre of
global gravity. I hope you agree with me?

G.   *Continue, Rakovsky, I beg you.*

R.   *.... Histographers and the masses, blinded by the*
shouts and the pomp of the French revolution, the
people, intoxicated by the fact that it had suc-
ceeded in taking all power from the King and the
privileged classes, did not notice how a small
group of mysterious, careful and insignificant

58

*people had taken possession of the real Royal power, the magical power, almost divine, which it obtained almost without knowing it. The masses did not notice that the power had been seized by others and that soon they had subjected them to a **slavery more cruel than the King, since the latter, in view of his religious and moral prejudices, was incapable of taking advantage of such a power.** So it came about that the supreme Royal power was taken over by persons, whose moral, intellectual and cosmopolitan qualities did allow them to use it. It is clear that these were people who had never been Christians, but cosmopolitans.*

*.... A great part of the money circulating, money for big affairs as representative of all national wealth, yes money - it was being issued by those few people about whom I had hinted. Titles, figures, cheques, promissory notes, endorsements, discounts, quotations, figures without end, flooded States like a waterfall..... They, being the most subtle psychologists, were able to gain even more without trouble, thanks to a lack of understanding. In addition to the immensely varied different forms of financial moneys, they created credit money with a view to making its volume close to infinite. And to give it the speed of sound.... **it is an abstraction, a being of thought, a figure, number; credit, faith....***

*Do you understand already?.... **Fraud, false moneys, given a legal standing.....** using other terminology, so that you should understand me. Banks, the Stock Exchanges and the whole world financial system - **is a gigantic machine for the purpose of bringing about unnatural scandals, to***

*force money to produce moneys - that is some-
thing that if it is a crime in economics then in
relation to finances **it is a crime against the crimi-
nal code, since it is usury**.... we see that usury still
exists, since even if the interest received is legal,
then **it invents and falsifies the non-existent capital**.... Bearing in mind that lawful interest is fixed
not on real capital but on non-existing capital, **the
interest is illegal by so many times as the fictional
capital is greater than the real one**.....*

*Imagine to yourself, if you can, a small number of
people having unlimited power through the possession of real wealth, and you will see that they
are the absolute dictators of the stock-exchange;
and as a result of this also **the dictators of production and distribution and also of work and con-
sumption**. If you have enough imagination then
multiply this by the global factor and you will see
its anarchical, moral and social influence, i.e.
revolutionary one.... Do you now understand?*

G.   *No, not yet.*

R.   *Obviously it is very difficult to understand miracles.*

G.   *Miracle?*

R.   *Yes, miracle. **Is it not a miracle that a wooden
bench has been transformed into a temple?** And
yet such a miracle has been seen by people a
thousand times, and they did not bat an eyelid,
during a whole century. Since this was an extraordinary miracle that the benches on which sat the
greasy usurers to trade in their moneys **have now
been converted into temples**, which stand magnifi-*

*cently at every corner of contemporary big towns,
with their heathen colonades, and crowds go there
with a faith which they are already not given by
heavenly gods, in order to bring assiduously their
deposits of all their possessions to the god of
money, who, they imagine, lives in the steel safes of
the bankers, and who is preordained, thanks to his
divine mission, **to increase the wealth to a meta-
physical infinity.***

G.   *This is the new religion...*

R.   *Religion, **yes, the religion of power.***

G.   *What do you pretend to?*

R.   ***I simply assert that they are revolutionaries objectively and subjectively, quite consciously.***

G.   *.... You must be mad?*

R.   *I, no... But you? Think a little. Why should not
these people have the impulse towards power,
towards full power? Just as it happens to you and
me.*

G.   *But if, according to you - and I think the same - they
already have global political, then what other
power do they want to possess?*

R.   *Power, if in reality it is absolute, can be only one.
The idea of the absolute excludes multiplicity.
..... Understand that is the only thing which they
have not yet reached....*

G.   *This is interesting at least as an example of insanity.*

R.   *Certainly, insanity in a lesser degree than in the
case of Lenin who dreamt of power over the whole
world in this attic in Switzerland, or the insanity of
Stalin, dreaming of the same thing during his exile
in a Siberian hut. **I think that dreams of such***

61

ambitions are much more natural for the mon-
eyed people, living in the skyscrapers of New
York.

G. *Let us conclude: Who are they?*

R. *You are so naive that you think that if I knew who "They" are, I would be here as a prisoner?*

G. *Why?*

R. *For the very simple reason, since he who is acquainted with them would not be put into a position in which he would be obliged to report on them.... This is an elementary rule of every intelligent conspiracy, which you must well understand.....*

*I think I shall not be wrong if I tell you that not one of "Them" is a person who occupies a political position or a position in the World Bank. As I understand, after the murder of Rathenau in Rapallo, they give political or financial positions only to intermediaries. Obviously to persons who are trustworthy and loyal, which can be guaranteed a thousand ways; thus one can assert that **bankers and politicians - are only men of straw.....** even though they occupy very high places **and are made to appear to be the authors of the plans which are carried out.***

G. *..... according to the information I have, you occupied a sufficiently high place in this conspiracy to have known much more. You do not know even a single one of them personally?*

R. *..... Mystics of pure power, who have become free from all vulgar trifles. I do not know if you understand me? Well, as to their place of resi-*

dence and names, I do not know them.... Imagine Stalin just now, in reality ruling the U.S.S.R., but not surrounded by stone walls, not having any personnel around him, and having the same guarantees for his life as any other citizen. By which means could he guard against attempts on his life? He is first of all a conspirator, however great his power; he is anonymous.

.... You know that according to the unwritten history known only to us, the founder of the First Communist International is indicated, of course secretly, as being Weishaupt..... he was ordered to found a secret organisation which was to provoke and push the French Revolution to go further than its political objectives with the aim of transforming it into a social revolution for the establishment of Communism. In those heroic times it was dangerous to mention Communism as an aim; from this derive the various precautions and secrets, which had to surround the Illuminati. More than a hundred years were required before a man could admit to being a Communist without danger of going to prison or being executed. This is more or less known. What is not known are the relations between Weishaupt and his followers with the first of the Rothschilds. The secret of the acquisition of wealth of the best known bankers could have been explained by the fact that they were the treasurers of this first Comintern. There is evidence that when the five brothers spread out to the five provinces of the financial empire of Europe, they had some secret help for the accumulation of these enormous sums; it is possible that they were the

first Communists from the Bavarian catacombs who were already spread all over Europe. But others say, and I think with better reason, that the Rothschilds were not the treasurers, but chiefs of that first secret Communism. The opinion is based on **the well-known fact that Marx and the highest chiefs of the First International - already the open one - and among them Herzen and Heine were controlled by Baron Lionel Rothschild,** *whose revolutionary portrait was done by D'Israeli the English Premier, who was his creature, and has been left to us. He described him in the character of Sidonia, a man who, according to the story, was a multimillionaire, knew and controlled spies, carbonari, freemasons, secret Jews, gypsies, revolutionaries, etc. etc. All this seems fantastic. But it has been proved that Sidonia is an idealised portrait of the son of Nathan Rothschild, which also can be deduced from that campaign which he raised against Tsar Nicholas in favour of Herzen. He won this campaign. If all that we can guess in the light of these facts is true, then, I think, we could even determine who invented the terrible machine of accumulation and anarchy, which is the Financial International. At the same time, I think he would be the same person who also created the Revolutionary International. It is an act of genius;* **to create with the help of Capitalism accumulation of the highest degree, to push the proletariat towards strikes, to sow hopelessness, and at the same time to create an organisation which must unite proletarians with the purpose of driving them into revolution. This is to**

*write the most majestic chapter of history. Even
more: remember the phrase of the mother of the
five Rothschilds brothers: "If my sons want it, then
there will be no war."* **This means that they were
the arbiters of peace and war, but not emperors.**
Are you capable of visualising **the fact of such a
cosmic importance?** *Is not war already a revolutionary function?* **War-the Commune. Since
that time every war was a giant step towards Communism.** *As if some mysterious force satisfied the
passionate wish of Lenin, which he had expressed
to Gorky. Remember 1905 - 1914. Do admit at
least that two of the three levers of power which
lead to Communism are not controlled and cannot
be controlled by the proletariat. Wars were not
brought about and were not controlled by either
the Third International or the U.S.S.R., which did
not yet exist at that time. Equally they cannot be
provoked and still less controlled by those small
groups of Bolsheviks who plod along in the emi-
gration, although they want war. This is quite
obvious The International and the U.S.S.R. have
even fewer possibilities for such immense accumulations of capital and the creation of national or
international anarchy in Capitalistic production.
Such an anarchy which is capable of forcing
people to burn huge quantities of foodstuffs, rather
than give them to starving people, and is capable
of that which Rathenau described in one of his
phrases, i.e.: "To bring about that half the world
will fabricate dung, and the other half will use it."
And after all, can the proletariat believe that it is
the cause of this inflation, growing in geometric*

progression, this devaluation, the constant acqui-
sition of surplus values and the accumulation of
financial capital, but not usury capital, and that as
the result of the fact that it cannot prevent the con-
stant lowering of its purchasing power, there takes
place the proletarization of the middle classes,
who are the true opponents of revolution. The
proletariat does not control the lever of economics
or the lever of war. But it is itself the third lever,
the only visible and demonstrable lever, which
carries out the final blow at the power of the
Capitalistic State and takes it over. Yes, they seize
it, if "They" yield it to them....

G. *.... if, as you claim, there is yet someone else's will*
and activity apart from the proletariat, then I want
you to indicate to me concretely a personal case.

R. *You require only one? Well, then listen to a small*
story: "They" isolated the Tsar diplomatically for
the Russo-Japanese War, and the United States
financed Japan; speaking precisely, this was done
by Jacob Schiff, the head of the bank of Kuhn, Loeb
and Co. which is the successor of the House of
Rothschild, whence Schiff originated. He had such
power that he achieved that States which had
colonial possessions in Asia supported the crea-
tion of the Japanese Empire, which was inclined
towards xenophobia; and Europe already feels
the effects of this zenophobia. From the prisoner-
of-war camps there came to Petrograd the best
fighters, trained as revolutionary agents; they
were sent there from America with the permission
of Japan, obtained through the persons who had
financed it. The Russo-Japanese War, thanks to

*the organised defeat of the Tsar's army, called
forth the revolution of 1905, which, though it was
premature, but was very nearly successful even if
it did not win, it still created the required political
condition for the victory of 1917. I shall say even
more. Have you read the biography of Trotzky?
Recall its first revolutionary period. He is still
quite a young man; after his flight from Siberia he
lived some time among the emigres in London,
Paris, and Switzerland; Lenin, Plekhanov, Martov and other chiefs look on him only as a promis-
ing newcomer. But he already dares during the
first split to behave independently, trying to become the arbiter of the reunion. In 1905 he is 25
years old and he returns to Russia alone, without
a party and without his own organisation. Read
the reports of the revolution of 1905 which have
not been "pruned" by Stalin; for example that of
Lunatcharsky, who was not a Trotzkyite. Trotzky
is the chief figure during the revolution in Petrograd. This is how it really was. Only he emerges
from it with increased popularity and influence.
Neither Lenin, nor Martov nor Plekanov acquire
popularity. They only keep it and even lose a little.
How and why there rises the unknown Trotzky,
gaining power by one move greater than that
which the oldest and most influential revolutionaries had? Very simple: he marries. Together with
him there arrives in Russia his wife - Sedova. Do
you know who she is? She is associated with Ziv-
otovsky, linked with the Bankers Warburg, part-
ners and relatives of Jacob Schiff, i.e. of that
financial group which as I said, had also financed*

the revolution of 1905. **Here is the reason why Trotzky, in one move, moves to the top of the revolutionary list.** *And here, too, you have the key to his real personality. Let us jump to 1914. Behind the back of the people who made the attempt on the Archduke there stands Trotzky, and that attempt provoked the European War. Do you really believe that the murder and the war – are simple coincidences?.... as had been said at one of the Zionist congresses by Lord Melchett. Analyse in the light of "non-coincidence" the development of the military action in Russia. "Defeatism" is an exemplary word. The help of the Allies and the Tsar was regulated and controlled with such skill that it gave the Allied ambassadors the right to make an argument of this and to get from Nicholas, thanks to his stupidity, suicidal advances, one after another. The mass of the Russian cannon fodder was immense, but not inexhaustible. A series of organised defeats led to the revolution. When the threat came from all sides, then a cure was found in the form of the establishment of a democratic republic - an "ambassadorial republic" as Lenin called it, i.e. this meant the elimination of any threat to the revolutionaries. But that is not yet all. Kerensky was to provoke the future advance at the cost of a very great deal of blood. He brings it about so that the democratic revolution should spread beyond its bounds. And even still more: Kerensky was to surrender the State fully to Communism, and he does it. Trotzky has the chance in an "unnoticed manner" to occupy the whole State apparatus. What a strange blindness? Well that is* the reality of the much praised October revolution. The Bolsheviks took that which "They" gave them.

G.   You dare to say that Kerensky was a collaborator of Lenin?

R.   Of Lenin - no. Of Trotzky - yes; it is more correct to say - a collaborator of "**Them**".

G.   An absurdity!

R.   You cannot understand.... precisely you? It surprises me. If you were to be a spy and, while hiding your identity, you were to attain the position of commander of the enemy fortress, then would you not open the gates to the attacking forces in whose service you were? You would not have become a prisoner who had experienced defeat? Would you not have been in danger of death during the attack on the fortress if one of the attackers, not knowing that your uniform is only a mask, would have taken you for an enemy? **Believe me: despite the statues and the mausoleum - Communism is indebted to Kerensky much more than to Lenin.**

G.   You want to say that Kerensky was a conscious and voluntary defeatist?

R.   Yes to me that is quite clear. Understand that I personally took part in all this. I shall tell you even more: Do you know who financed the October revolution? "**They**" financed it, in particular through those same bankers who had financed Japan in 1905, i.e. Jacob Schiff, and the brothers Warburg; that means through the great banking constellations, through one of the five banks who are members of the Federal Reserve, through the bank of Kuhn, Loeb and Co.; here there took part also other American and European bankers, such

*as Guggenheim, Hanquer, Breitung, Aschber, the
"Nye-Banken" of Stockholm. I was there "by
chance", there in Stockholm, and participated in
the transmission of funds. Until Trotzky arrived I
was the only person who was an intermediary from
the revolutionary side. But at last Trotzky came; I
must underline that the Allies had expelled him
from France for being a defeatist. And the same
Allies released him so that he could be a defeatist
in allied Russia.... "Another chance." Who arranged it? The same people who had succeeded
that Lenin passed through Germany. Yes, "**They**"
were able to get the defeatist Trotzky out of a
Canadian camp to England and send him on to
Russia, giving him the chance to pass freely through
all the Allied controls; others of "**Them**" - a
certain Rathenau - accomplishes the journey of
Lenin through enemy Germany. If you will under-
take the study of the history of the revolution and
civil war without prejudices, and will use all your
enquiring capabilities, which you know how to
apply to things much less important and less obvious, then when you study information in their
totality and also study separate details right up to
anecdotal happenings, you will meet with a whole
series of "**amazing chances.**"*

G. *Alright, let us accept the hypothesis that not everything was simply a matter of luck. What deductions
do you make here for practical results?*

R. *Let me finish this little story, and then we shall both
arrive at conclusions. From the time of his arrival
in Petrograd Trotzky was openly received by Lenin.
As you know sufficiently well, during the interval*

between the two revolutions there had been deep differences between them. All is forgotten and Trotzky emerges as the master of his trade in the matter of the triumph of the revolution, whether Stalin wants this or not. Why? This secret is known to the wife of Lenin - Krupskaya. She knows who Trotzky is in fact; it is she who persuaded Lenin to receive Trotzky. If he had not received him then Lenin would have remained blocked up in Switzerland; this alone had been for him a serious reason, and in addition he knew that Trotzky provided money and helped to get a colossal international assistance; a proof of this was the sealed train. Furthermore it was the result of Trotzky's work, and not of the iron determination of Lenin that there was the unification round the insignificant party of the Bolsheviks of the whole Left-wing revolutionary camp, the social revolutionaries and the anarchists. It was not for nothing that the real party of the "non-party" Trotzky was the ancient "Bund" of the Jewish proletariat, from which emerged all the Moscow revolutionary branches, and to whom it gave 90% of its leaders; not the official and well known Bund, but the secret Bund, which had been infiltrated into all the Socialist parties, the leaders of which were almost all under its control.

G.   *And Kerensky too?*

R.   *Kerensky too.... and also some other leaders who were not Socialists, the leaders of the bourgeois political fractions.*

G.   *How is that?*

R.   *Masonry, you forget about the role of freemasonry*

71

in the first phase of the democratic bourgeois revolution?

At this point there followed a long statement on the role of Masonry in the revolution and the reason for all its secret oaths.

G. *Do you want to say that the freemasons have to die at the hands of the revolution which has been brought about with their co-operation.*

R. *Exactly so. You have formulated a truth which is veiled by a great secret. I am a Mason, you already know about that. Well, I shall tell you this great secret, which they promise to disclose to a mason in one of the higher degrees, but which is not disclosed to him either in the 25th, nor the 33rd, nor the 93rd, nor any other high level of any ritual. It is clear that I know this not as a Freemason, but as one who belongs to "Them"....*

....But since the Communist revolution has in mind the liquidation, as a class, of the whole bourgeoisie, the physical destruction of all bourgeois political rulers, it follows that the real secret of masonry - is the suicide of freemasonry as an organisation, and the physical suicide of every more important mason. You can, of course, understand that such an end, which is being prepared for every mason, fully deserves the secrecy, decorativeness and the inclusion of yet another whole series of secrets, with a view to concealing the real one. If one day you were to be present at some future revolution, then do not miss the opportunity of observing the gestures of surprise and the expression of stupidity on the face of some Freemason at the moment

> *when he realises that he must die at the hands of the revolutionaries. How he screams and wants that one should value his services to the revolution! It is a sight at which one can die.... but of laughter.*

G. *And you still deny the inborn stupidity of the bourgeoise?*

R. *I deny it in the bourgeoisie as a class, but not in certain sectors. The existence of madhouses does not prove universal madness. Freemasonry is also a madhouse, but at literty. But I continue further: the revolution has been victorious: ....There arises the first problem: peace,*

At this point Rakovsky describes the fierce in-fighting at the top of the Party. He tells how Stalin planned the murder of Lenin, that Trotzky was groomed by **"Them"** to succeed Lenin. Then at the crucial moment when he was to take over, Trotzky became too ill to act. Stalin moved fast. Trotzky's followers then sided with Stalin pretending to be more Stalinist than Stalin. Stalin could read their thoughts but bided his time for revenge.

The Plan

G. *That is enough, Rakovsky. You are not here to make Trotzkyist propaganda. Will you at last get to something concrete?*

R. *It is clear that I shall, but not before I have reached the point at which you will have formulated for yourself an at least superficial conception concerning "Them", with whom you will have to reckon in practice and in concrete reality*

....Our failures, which get worse every year, prevent the immediate carrying out of that which

73

"They" have prepared in the after-war period for the further leap of the revolution forward. The Versailles Treaty quite inexplicable for the politicians and economists of all nations, insofar as nobody could give its projection, as the most decisive precondition for the revolution.... The Versailles reparations and economic limitations were not determined by the advantages of the individual nations. Their arithmetical absurdity was so obvious that even the most outstanding economists of the victorious countries soon exposed this....

Hunger and unemployment on both sides, all this were the first results of Versailles....

More than thirty million unemployed in Europe and U.S.A. alone. Well, did not the Versailles Peace Treaty and its League of Nations serve as a revolutionary pre-condition?

We do not wish that the great preconditions which we had created at Versaille for the triumph of the Communist revolution in the world, which, as you see, have become a gigantic reality, would serve the purpose of bringing victory to Stalin's Bonapartism.... Everything would have been different if in this case Trotzky had been the dictator of the U.S.S.R.; that would have meant that "They" would have been the chiefs of International Communism.

G. *But surely Fascism is totally anti-Communist, as in relation to the Trotzkyist and the Stalinist Communism.... and if the power which you ascribe to "Them" is so great, how is it that they were unable to avoid this?*

74

T.   *Because it were precisely "They" who gave Hitler the possibility of triumphing.*

G.   *You exceed all the boundaries of absurdity.*

R.   *....Listen to me.... "They" saw in the end that Stalin cannot be overthrown by a coup d' etat, and their historical experience suggested to them the decision of a repetition (repris) with Stalin of that which had been done with the Tsar. There was here one difficulty, which seemed to us insuperable. In the whole of Europe there was not a single aggressor State. Not one of them was geographically well placed and had an army sufficient for an attack on Russia. If there was no such country, then "They" had to create it. Only Germany had the corresponding population and positions suitable for an attack on the U.S.S.R., and it was capable of defeating Stalin; you can understand that the Weimar republic had not been invented as an aggressor either politically or economically; on the contrary, it was suited to an invasion. On the horizon of a hungry Germany there sparkled the meteor of Hitler. A pair of penetrating eyes fixed their attention on it. The world was the witness to his lightning rise.... His rise, uninterruptedly increasing in extent, took place as the result of the Revolutionary-Communist economy of Versailles. Versailles had had in mind not the creation of preconditions for the triumph of Hitler, but for the proletarisation of Germany, for unemployment and hunger, as the result of which there should have triumphed the Communist Revolution....*

....In 1929, when the National-Socialist Party began to experience a crisis of growth and it had insufficient financial resources, "They" sent their ambassador there. I even know his name. It was one of the Warburgs. In direct negotiations with Hitler they agreed as to the financing of the National-Socialist Party, and the latter received in a couple of years millions of dollars, sent to it from Wall Street, and Millions of marks from German financiers through Schacht; the upkeep of the S.A. and S.S. and also the financing of the elections which took place, which gave Hitler power, are done on the Dollars and marks sent by "Them" ....

Do you not observe the general sympathy of the Versailles wolves, who limit themselves to a weak growl? Is this yet another chance, accident?....

G. *All right, let us talk in the form of a supposition. What will you say?*

R. *....We are not at the moment interested in the attack on the U.S.S.R., since the fall of Stalin would presuppose the destruction of Communism....*

G. *Splendid, the solution....*

R. *First of all we must make sure that there would be no potential possibility of an attack by Hitler.*

G. *If, as you confirm, it were "They" who made him Fuhrer, then they have power over him and he must obey them.*

R. *....If it is true that "They" financed Hitler, then that does not mean that they disclosed to him their existence and their aims. The ambassador Warburg presented himself under a false name and Hitler did not even guess his race, he also lied regarding whose representative he was.... our aim*

76

*was to provoke a war.... **and Hitler was war.** Do you now understand?*

G. *I understand. Consequently I do not see any other way of stopping him as the creation of a coalition of the U.S.S.R. with the democratic nations, which would be capable of frightening Hitler. I think he will not be able to attack simultaneously all the countries of the world. The most would be - each in turn.*

R. *Does not a simpler solution come to your mind.... I would say - a counter-revolutionary one?*

G. *To avoid war against the U.S.S.R.?*

R. *Shorten the phrase by half.... and repeat with me "avoid war".... is that not an absolutely counter-revolutionary thing? Every sincere Communist imitating his idol, Lenin, and the greatest revolutionary strategists must always wish for war. Nothing is so effective in bringing nearer the victory of revolution as war. This is a Marxist-Leninist dogma which you must preach.... the transformation into which Stalin has fallen subjects the revolution to the State, and not the State to the revolution....*

G. *Your hate of Stalin blinds you and you contradict yourself. Have we not agreed that an attack on the U.S.S.R. would not be welcome?*

R. *But why should war be necessarily against the Soviet Union?*

G. *But on what other country could Hitler make war? It is sufficiently clear that he would direct his attack on the U.S.S.R., of this he speaks in his speeches. What further proof do you need?*

R. *If you, the people from the Kremlin, consider it to*

*be quite definite and not debatable, **then why did
you provoke the Civil War in Spain.** Do not tell me
that it was done for purely revolutionary reasons....*

*there is yet a second point of agreement between
us: the first - the first - that there must be no war
against the U.S.S.R.; the second - that it would be
well to provoke it between the bourgeois States.*

G.   *Yes, I agree. Is that your personal opinion, or
"Theirs"?*

R.   *I express it as my opinion. I have no power and no
contact with **"Them"**, but I can confirm that in
these two points it coincides with the view of the
Kremlin.... If I had the time to explain their full
scheme, then you would already know about the
reasons for their approval. At the present moment
I shall condense them to three:*

G.   *Just which?*

R.   *One is that which I had already mentioned. Hitler,
this uneducated and elementary man, has restored,
thanks to his natural intuition and even against the
technical opinion of Schacht, an economic system
of a very dangerous kind. Being illiterate in all
economic theories and being guided only by necessity, he removed, as we had done it in the U.S.S.R.,
the private and international capital. That means
that he took over for himself the privilege of
manufacturing money, and not only physical
moneys, but also financial ones, he took over the
untouched machinery of falsification **and put it to
work for the benefit of the State. He exceeded us,**
as we, having abolished it in Russia, replaced it
merely by this crude apparatus called State Capi-*

talism; this was a very expensive triumph in view of the necessities of pre-revolutionary demagogy.... Here I give you two real facts for comparison. I shall even say that Hitler had been lucky; he had almost no gold, and for that reason he was not tempted to create a gold reserve. Insofar as he only possessed a full monetary guarantee of technical equipment and colossal working capacity of the Germans, his "gold reserve" was technical capacity and work.... something so completely counter-revolutionary that, as you already see, he has by means of magic, as it were, radically eliminated unemployment among more than seven million technicians and workers.

G.   *Thanks to increased re-armament.*

R.   *What does your re-armament give?* **If Hitler reached this despite all the bourgeois economists who surround him, then he was quite capable, in the absence of the danger of war, of applying his system also to peaceful production....** *Are you capable of imagining what would have come of this system if he had infected a number of other States and brought about the creation of a period of autarky.... For example the Commonwealth. If you can, then imagine, its counter-revolutionary functions.... The danger is not yet inevitable, as we have had luck in that Hitler restored his system not according to some previous theory,* **but empirically, and he did not make any formulations of a scientific kind.*** *This means that insofar as he did*

* *The problem of a scientific formulation of this question and the propounding of a corresponding programme has engaged the active attention of the publishers of Red Symphony and their associates for some years. Major Douglas in Social Credit has also given a scientific formulation.*

not think in the light of a deductive process based on intelligence, he has no scientific terms or a formulated doctrine; yet there is a hidden danger as **at any moment there can appear, as the consequence of deduction, a formula. This is very serious.** *Much more so than all the external and cruel factors in National-Socialism.* **We do not attack it in our propaganda as it could happen that through theoretical polemics we would ourselves provoke a formulation and systematization of this so decisive economic doctrine. There is only one solution - war.**

G.   *And the second motive?*

R.   *....**the need for the destruction of nationalism is alone worth a war in Europe.***

G.   *You have set out one economic and one political reason. Which is the third?*

R.   *That is easy to guess.* **We have yet another reason, a religious one.** *Communism cannot be the victor if it will not have suppressed the still living Christianity. History speaks very clearly about this; the permanent revolution required seventeen centuries in order to achieve its first partial victory - by means of the creation of the first split in Christendom.* **In reality Christianity is our only real enemy,** *since all the political and economic phenomena in the bourgeois States are only its consequences. Christianity, controlling the individual, is capable of annulling the revolutionary projection of the neutral Soviet or atheistic State by choking it and, as we see it in Russia, things have reached the point of the creation of that spiritual nihilism which is dominant in the ruling masses,*

*which have, nevertheless, remained Christian:
this obstacle has not yet been removed during
twenty years of Marxism. Let us admit in relation
to Stalin that towards religion he was not bonapar-
tistic. We would not have done more than he and
would have acted in the same way. And if Stalin
had dared, like Napoleon, to cross the Rubicon of
Christianity, **then his nationalism and counter-
revolutionary power would have been increased
a thousand fold.** In addition, if this had happened
then so radical a difference would have made quite
impossible any collaboration in anything between
us and him, even if this were to be only temporary
and objective.... like the one you can see becoming
apparent to us.*

G. *And so I personally consider that you have given a
definition of three fundamental points, on the basis
of which a plan can be made. ....Now continue to
follow the general lines of your plan.*

R. *I am responsible for the interpretation of those
preceding points in the sense in which "They"
understand them, but I admit that "They" may
consider another plan to be more effective for the
attainment of the three aims, and one quite unlike
that which I shall now set out. Bear that in mind.*

G. *Very well, we shall bear it in mind. Please speak.*

R. *We shall simplify. Insofar as the object is missing
for which the German military might had been
created - to give us power in the U.S.S.R. - the aim
now is to bring about an advance on the fronts and
to direct the Hitlerist advance not towards the
East, but the West.*

81

G.   *Exactly. Have you thought of the practical plan of realization?*

R.   *I had more than enough time for that at the Lubianka. So look: if there were difficulties in finding mutually shared points between us and all else took its normal course, then the problem comes down to again trying to establish that in which there is similarity between Hitler and Stalin.*

....With Hitler and with Stalin one can find common ground, as, being very different people, they have the same roots; if Hitler is sentimental to a pathological degree, but Stalin is normal, yet both of them are egoists: neither one of them is an idealist, and for the reason both of them are bonapartists, i.e. classical imperialists. And if just that is the position, then it is already not difficult to find common ground between them. Why not, it proved possible between one Tsarina and one Prussian King....

G.   *Rakovsky, you are incorrigible....*

R.   *You do not guess? If Poland was the point of union between Catherine and Frederick - the Tsarina of Russia and the King of Germany at that time, then why cannot Poland serve as a reason for the finding of common ground between Hitler and Stalin? In Poland the persons of Hitler and Stalin can coincide, and also the historical Tsarist - Bolshevik and Nazi lines. Our line, "**Their**" line - also, as Poland is a Christian State and, **what makes the matter even more complex, a Catholic one.***

G.   *And what follows from the fact of such a treble coincidence?*

R. *If there is common ground then there is a possibility of agreement.*

G. *Between Hitler and Stalin? ....Absurd! Impossible.*

R. **In politics there are neither absurdities, nor the impossible.**

G. *Let us imagine, as a hypothesis: Hitler and Stalin advance on Poland.*

R. *Permit me to interrupt you; an attack can be called forth only by the following: war or peace. You must admit it.*

G. *Well, and so what?*

R. *Do you consider that England and France, with their worse armies and aviation, in comparison with Hitler's, can attack the united Hitler and Stalin?*

G. *Yes, that seems to me to be very difficult.... unless America....*

R. *Let us leave the United States aside for the moment. Will you agree with me that as the result of the attack of Hitler and Stalin on Poland there can be no European war?*

G. *You argue logically; it would seem impossible.*

R. *In that case an attack or war would be useless. It would not call forth the mutual destruction of the bourgeois States: the Hitlerist threat to the U.S.S.R. would continue in being after the division of Poland since theoretically both Germany and the U.S.S.R. would have been strengthened to the same extent. In practice Hitler to a greater extent, since the U.S.S.R. does not need more land and raw materials for its strengthening, but Hitler does need them.*

G. *This is a correct view.... but I can see no other solution.*

R. *No, there is a solution.*

G. *Which?*

R. *That the democracies should attack and not attack the aggressor.*

G. *What are you saying, what hallucination! Simultaneously to attack and not to attack.... That is something absolutely impossible.*

R. *You think so? Calm down.... Are there not two aggressors? Did we not agree that there will be no advance just because there are two? Well.... What prevents the attack on one of them?*

G. *What do you want to say by that?*

R. **Simply that the democracies will declare war only on one aggressor, and that will be Hitler.**

G. *Yes, but that is an unfounded hypothesis.*

R. *An hypothesis, but having a foundation. Consider: each State will have to fight with a coalition of enemy States has as its main strategical objective to destroy them separately one after another. This rule is so well known that proofs are superfluous. So, agree with me that there are no obstacles to the creation of such conditions. I think that the question that Stalin will not consider himself aggrieved in case of an attack on Hitler is already settled. Is that not so? In addition geography imposes this attitude, and for that reason strategy also. **However stupid France and England may be in preparing to fight simultaneously against two countries,** one of which wants to preserve its neutrality, while the other, even being alone, represents for them a serious opponent, from where* *and from which side could they carry out an attack on the U.S.S.R.? They have not got a common border; unless they were to advance over the Himalayas.... Yes, there remains the air front, but with what forces and from where could they invade Russia? In comparison with Hitler they are weaker in the air. All the arguments I have mentioned are no secret and are well known. As you see, all is simplified to a considerable extent.*

G. *You forget about the United States.*

R. *In a moment you will see that I have not forgotten, I shall limit myself to the investigation of their function in the preliminary programme, which occupies us at present, and I shall say that America will not be able to force France and England to attack Hitler and Stalin simultaneously. In order to attain that, the United States would have to enter the war from the first day. But that is impossible. In the first place because America did not enter a war formerly and never will do so, if it is not attacked.* **Its rulers can arrange that they will be attacked, if that will suit them.** *Of that I can assure you. In those cases when provocation was not successful, and the enemy did not react to it, aggression was invented. In their first international war, the war against Spain, of the defeat of which they were sure,* **they invented an aggression, or, more correctly, "They" invented it....** *Now this splendid American technique which I welcome at any moment, is subject to one condition: that aggression should take place at a suitable moment, i.e. the moment required by the United States who are being attacked; that means* *then, when they will have the arms. Does this condition exist now? It is clear that it does not. In America there are at present a little less than one hundred thousand men under arms and a middling aviation: it has only an imposing fleet. But you can understand that, having it, it can not persuade its allies to decide on an attack on the U.S.S.R., since England and France have preponderance only at sea. I have also proved to you that from that side there can be no change in the comparative strengths of the forces.*

G.   *....I ask you again to explain once more the technical realisation.....*

R.   *....given the coincidence of the interests of Stalin and Hitler with regard to an attack on Poland, all comes down to the formalization of this full similarity of aims and to make a pact about a double attack.*

G.   *And you think this is easy?*

R.   *Frankly, no. Here we need a diplomacy which is more experienced than that of Stalin.... At the present moment I would suggest to the one who begins the talks, that they should be strictly confidential, but with great open sincerity. Given a whole wall of various prejudices only truthfulness can deceive Hitler.... With Hitler one must play a clean game concerning the concrete and most immediate questions. It is necessary to show him that the game is not played in order to provoke him into war on two fronts....*

Stalin will have to be generous with the preliminary supplies which Hitler will demand, chiefly oil.... Thousands of further questions will arise, of a similar character, which will have to be solved so that Hitler, seeing in practice that we only want to occupy our part of Poland, would be quite certain of that. And insofar as in practice it should be just like that, he will be deceived by the truth.

G.   *But in what, in this case, is there a deception?*

R.   *I shall give you a few minutes of time so that you yourself can discover just in what there is a deception of Hitler. But first I want to stress, and you should take note, that the plan which I have indicated here, is logical and normal and I think that one can achieve that the Capitalistic States will destroy each other, if one brings about a clash of their two wings: the fascist and the bourgeois. I repeat that the plan is logical and normal. As you have already been able to see, there is no intervention here of mysterious or unusual factors. In short, in order that one should be able to realize the plan, **"Their"** intervention is not required. Now I should like to guess your thoughts; are you not now thinking that it would be stupid to waste time on proving the unprovable existence and power held by **"Them"**, Is that not so?*

G.   *You are right.*

R.   *Be frank with me. Do you really not observe their intervention? I informed you, wanting to help you, that their intervention exists and is decisive, and for that reason the logic and naturalness of the plan are only appearances.... Is it really true that you do not see **"Them"**?*

G.   *Speaking sincerely, no.*

R.   *The logic and naturalness of my plan is only an ap-*

*pearance. It would be natural and logical that Hitler and Stalin would inflict defeat on each other. For the democracies that would be a simple and easy thing, if they would have to put forward such an aim; for them it would be enough that Hitler should be permitted, make note "permitted" to attack Stalin. Do not tell me that Germany could be defeated. If the Russian distances and the dreadful fear of Stalin and his henchmen of the Hitlerite axe and the revenge of their victims will not be enough in order to attain the military exhaustion of Germany, then there will be no obstacles to the democracies, seeing that Stalin is losing strength, beginning to help him wisely and methodically, continuing to give that help until the complete exhaustion of both armies. In reality that would be easy, natural and logical, if those mo-tives and aims which are put forward by the de-mocracies, and which most of their followers be-lieve to be true ones, and not what they are in reality - pretexts. There is only one aim, one single aim: the triumph of Communism: **it is not Moscow which will impose its will on the democracies, but New York, not the "Comintern", but the "Capin-tern" on Wall Street.** Who other than he could have been able to impose on Europe such an obvious and absolute contradiction? What force can lead it towards complete suicide? Only one force is able to do this: money. **Money is power and the sole power.***

G.   *....You assert that "They" hinder or will hinder a German-Soviet War, which is logical from the point of view of the Capitalists. Have I explained it correctly?*

R. *Yes, precisely so.*

G. *....In the face of a new situation you only advise that Hitler and Stalin should sign a pact and divide Poland. I ask you how can we obtain a guarantee that, having the pact, or not having it, carrying out, or not carrying out the partition, Hitler will not attack the U.S.S.R.?*

R. *This cannot be guaranteed.*

G. *Then why go on talking?*

R. *....either there will be an attack on Stalin, or there will come the realisation of the plan I have indicated, according to which the European Capitalistic States will destroy each other.... If Stalin wants to survive, then he will be forced to realise the plan which has been proposed by me and ratified by "**Them**".*

G. *But if he refuses?*

R. *That will be impossible for him. The expansion and rearmament of Germany will continue. When Stalin will be faced by this gigantic threat.... then what will he do? This will be dictated to him by his own instinct of self-preservation.*

G. *It seems that events must develop only according to the orders indicated by "**Them**".*

R. *....**Reject the wrong thought that you are the arbiters in the given situation, since "They" are the arbiters.***

G. *....Therefore we must deal with shadows?*

R. *But are facts shadows? The international situation will be extraordinary, but not shadowy; it is real and very real. This is not a miracle; here is predetermined the future policy? do you think this is the work of shadows?*

G.   *....let us assume that your plan is accepted.... But we must have something tangible, personal, in order to be able to carry out negotiations.*

R.   *For example?*

G.   *Some person with powers of attorney and representation.*

R.   *But for what? Just for the pleasure of becoming acquainted with him? For the pleasure of a talk? Bear in mind that the assumed person, in case of his appearance, will not present you with credentials, with seals and crests, and will not wear a diplomatic uniform, at least a man from "Them"; if he were to say something or promise, then it will have no juridical force or meaning as a pact.... Understand that "They" are not a State; "They" are that which the International was before 1917, that which it still is: nothing and at the same time everything. ....Such pacts as the pact of Lenin with the German General Staff, as the pact of Trotzky with "Them" - are realised without written documents and without signatures. The only guarantee of their execution is rooted in the circumstance, that the carrying out of that which has been agreed, is profitable for the parties to the pact, this guarantee is the sole reality in the pact, however great may be its importance.*

G.   *From what would you begin in the present case?*

R.   *Simple; I should begin already from tomorrow to sound out Berlin....*

G.   *In order to agree about the attack on Poland?*

R.   *I would not begin with that.... I would display my willingness to yield.... I would soft-pedal in Spain.... then I would drop a hint about Poland, nothing compromising, but enough so that a part of the German High Command would have some arguments to put before Hitler.*

G. *And nothing more.*

R. *For the beginning, nothing more; this is already a big diplomatic task*

G. *....I have not for a single moment experienced the temptation to consider the German-Soviet pact to be something realizable.*

R. *International events will force with irrestible strength....*

G. *....Consider something concrete, something which I could put forward as a proof of your veracity and credibility....*

R. *....if someone, even in a most official manner, were to have a talk with some very important person?*

G. *It seems to me that this would be something real.*

R. *But with whom?*

G. *This is only my personal opinion, Rakovsky. You had mentioned concrete persons, big financiers; if I remember correctly you had spoken about a certain Schiff, for example; then you mentioned another who had been a go-between with Hitler for the purpose of financing him. There are also politicians.... who belong to "Them" or, if you like, serve "Them".... Do you know someone?*

R. *....I have already told you that I do not know who is a part of "Them", but have assurances from a person who must have know "Them".*

G. *From whom?*

R. *From Trotzky....*

G. *....The most important thing is to get proofs that you spoke the truth.... If you succeed in this, then*

*I could nearly give you fairly solid assurances of
saving your life....in the contrary case I answer for
nothing.*

R.   *In the end I shall take the risk. Do you know if
Davis is at present in Moscow? yes, the Ambassador of the United States.*

G.   *I think he is; he should have returned.*

R.   *Only an exceptional situation gives me the right, as
I see it, against the rules, to make use of an official
intermediary.*

G.   *Therefore we can think that **the American Government is behind all this....***

R.   *Behind - no, **under all this....***

G.   *Roosevelt?*

R.   *....Remember the morning of the 24th October,
1929. The time will come when this day will be for
the history of the revolution more important than
October, 1917. On the day of the 24th October
there took place the crash of the New York Stock
Exchange, the beginning of the so-called "depression," a real revolution. The four years of the
Government of Hoover - are years of revolutionary progress: 12 and 15 millions on strike. In
February, 1933 there takes place the last stroke of
the crisis with the closing of the banks. It is difficult
to do more than capital did in order to break the
"classical American," who was still on his industrial bases, and in the economic respect enslaved
by Wall Street....*

*Although the power of money is political power,
but before that it had only been used indirectly, but
now the power of money was to be transformed
into direct power. The man through whom they*

made use of such power was Franklin Roosevelt.
Have you understood? Take note of the follow-
ing: In that year 1929, the first year of the Ameri-
can Revolution, in February Trotzky leaves
Russia; the crash takes place in October.... The
financing of Hitler is agreed in July, 1929. You
think that all this was by chance? The four years
of the rule of Hoover were used for the prepara-
tion of the seizure of power in the United States
and the U.S.S.R.; there by means of a financial
revolution, and here with the help of war and the
defeat which was to follow. Could some novel
with great imagination be more obvious to you.
You can understand that the execution of the
plan on such a scale requires a special man, who
can direct the executive power in the United
States, who has been predetermined to be the
organizing and deciding force. That man was
Franklin and Eleanor Roosevelt. And permit me
to say that this two-sexed being is not simply
irony. He had to avoid any possible Delilah.

G. *Is Roosevelt one of "Them"?*

R. *I do not know if he is one of "Them," or is only*
subject to "Them." I think he was conscious of his
mission, but cannot assert whether he obeyed
under duress or blackmail, or he was one of those
who rule; it is true that he carried out his mission,
realised all the actions which had been assigned to
him accurately. Do not ask me more....

G. *In case it should be decided to approach Davis, in*
which form would you do it?
....If it were to depend on me, then I would try. But
do you believe that the delegate....?

R. *Yes, I believe.... note one detail: the appointment*

93

*of Davis became known in November, 1936; we must assume that Roosevelt thought of sending him much sooner and with that in mind began preliminary steps; we all know that the consideration of the matter and the official explanations of the appointment take more than two months. Apparently his appointment was agreed in August.... And what happened in August? In August Zinoviev and Kemenev were shot. I am willing to swear that his appointment was made for the purpose of a new involvement of "**Them**" in the politics of Stalin. Yes, I certainly think so. With what an inner excitement must he have travelled, seeing how one after another there fall the chiefs of the opposition in the "purges" which follow one another. Do you know if he was present at the trial of Radeck?*

G.   *Yes.*

R.   *You will see him. Have a talk with him. He expects it already for many months.*

G.   *This night we must finish; but before we part I want to know something more. Let us assume that all this is true, and all will be carried out with full success. "**They**" will put forward definite conditions. Guess what they might be?*

R.   *This is not difficult to assume. The first condition will be the ending of the executions of the Communists, that means the Trotzkyists as you call them. ....they will demand the establishment of several zones of influence, as I had mentioned. The boundaries which will have to divide the formal Communism from the real one. That is the most important condition. There will be mutual concessions for mutual help for a time, while the plan lasts, being carried out. You will see for example the paradoxical phenomenon that a whole crowd of people, enemies of Stalin, will help him; no they will not necessarily be proletarians, nor will they be professional spies. There will appear influential persons at all levels of society, even very high ones, who will help the Stalinist formal Communism when it becomes if not real, then at least objective Communism. Have you understood me?*

G.   *A little: you wrap up such things in such impenetrable casuistry.*

R.   *....It is known that Marxism was called Hegelian. So this question was vulgarised. Hegelian idealism is a widespread adjustment to an uninformed understanding in the West of the natural mysticism of Baruch Spinosa. "They" are spinosists: perhaps the matter is the other way round, i.e. that spinosism is "Them," in so far as he is only a version adequate to the epoch of "Their" own philosophy, which is a much earlier one, standing on a much higher level. ....In Moscow there is Communism, in New York Capitalism. It is all the same as a thesis and anti-thesis. Analyze both. Moscow is subjective Communism, but Capitalism - objective - State Capitalism. New York: Capitalism subjective, but Communism objective. A personal synthesis, truth: the Financial International, the Capitalist-Communist one. "They."*

The meeting lasted six hours. As is well known, Stalin followed the advice of Rakovsky. There was a pact with Hitler. And the Second World War served solely the interests of the revolution. The secret of these changes of policy can be understood from a further conversation between Gabriel and Dr. Landowsky. Here are some extracts from it:

G.   *Do you remember the conversation with Rakovsky.... Do you know he was not condemned to death.... You need not be surprised that Comrade Stalin had thought it to be wise to try that apparently unlikely plan....*

D.   *I remember everything rather well. Do not forget that I heard the conversation twice, then both times I wrote it, and in addition I translated it.... May I find out if you know the people Rakovsky called* **"Them"**?

G.   *....We do not know for sure who* **"They"** *are, but at the last moment there was confirmed a great deal of what Rakovsky had told; for example it is true that Hitler was financed by the Wall Street bankers. Much else is also true. All these months during which I have not seen you, I devoted to an investigation, connected with Rakovsky's information. It is true that I was not able to establish just which people are such remarkable personages, but it is a fact, that there is a kind of entourage which consists of financiers, politicians, scientists, and even ecclesiastical persons of high rank, wealth and power, who occupy high places; if one is to judge their position (mostly as intermediaries) by the results, then it seems strange and inexplicable, at least in the light of ordinary conceptions.... since in fact they have a great similarity with the ideas of Communism. Of course with very special Communist ideas. But let us leave all these questions aside, concerning complexion, line and profile; objectively, as Rakovsky would have said,* *they, imitating Stalin blindly in actions and errors, are building Communism. They followed the advice of Rakovsky almost to the letter. There was nothing concrete, but there was no refusal and no tearing of mantles. On the contrary, they displayed great attention to everything. **The Ambassador Davis** carefully hinted at the past trials and even went so far as to hint that much would be gained in the public opinion in America, in case of an amnesty for Rakovsky in the near future. He was well watched during the trials in March, which is natural. He was himself present at all of them; we did not allow him to bring any technicians so as to prevent any "telegraphing" with the accused. He is not a professional diplomat and does not know the specific techniques. He was obliged to look on, trying with his eyes to say much, as I thought; we think that he raised the spirits of Rosenholz and of Rakovsky. The latter confirmed the interest which had been displayed at the trial by Davis and confessed that he made him a secret sign of Masonic greeting.*

There is yet another strange matter, which cannot be falsified. On the 2nd March at dawn there was received a radio message from some very powerful station: "Amnesty or the Nazi danger will increase".... The radiogramme was enciphered in the cypher of our own Embassy in London. You can understand that was something very important!

Dr.   *But the threat was not real?*

G.   *How not? On the 12th March there ended the*

*debates of the Supreme Tribunal and at 9 in the
evening the Tribunal began its considerations.
And on that same day of the 12th March, at 5.30
o'clock a.m. Hitler ordered his armoured divisions to enter Austria. Of course this was a
military promenade! Were there sufficient reasons for thinking about that? Or we had to be so
stupid as to consider the greetings of Davis, the
radiogramme, the cypher, the coincidence of the
invasion with the verdict, and also the silence of
Europe as being only accidental chances? No, in
fact we did not see "Them," but we heard their
voice and understood their language.*

George Knupffer, who wrote "The Struggle for World
Power" and who translated this document into English com-
menting on it says:

*....This is one of the most important political docu-
ments of the century. Many of us have known the
facts here brought out for decades, but for the first
time we get a brilliant, detailed statement from an
Insider. Obviously Rakovsky was one of "Them."
Both the internal evidence of this document, as
well as the circumstance that all subsequent events
went exactly according to the formulae indicated,
proves the truth of the story. This book should be
essential reading for all who wish to know what is
happening, and why, throughout the world, and
also what alone can be done to stop the conquests
of the revolution:
the power of monetary emission must be returned
to the States everywhere. If that is not done in time,
Communism will win.*

The Show Trials

The show trials of Rakovsky and 20 others began on March 2, 1938. Note well the words of Gabriel to Dr. Landowsky:

"There is yet another strange matter, which cannot be falsified. On 2nd March at dawn, there was received a radio message from some very powerful station:

Amnesty or the Nazi danger will increase.

The Radiogramme was encyphered in the cypher of our own embassy in London. You can understand that was very important."

The London Times gave full cover to the trials. Its correspondent reporting from Riga on March 2 stated

The Trial of the 21 Communists which (as reported on Page 14) has brought a surprise: M. Trotsky and several of the most important prisoners are charged with being British spies employed directly by the Intelligence Service.

According to the indictment they worked also for Germany and Japan. M. Trotzky is alleged to have received employment in the British Intelligence Service in 1926 and to have worked for five years previously as a spy and secret agent for Germany. M.Rakovsky is also accused of entering the Japanese Secret Service during his mission to Tokyo as Head of the Soviet Red Cross Delegation in 1934.....

This is positive proof of the degree that Rakovsky's fate and blueprint for war were being tuned to the events taking place at the Show Trials. The Trial actually started on the day that the signal "Amnesty or ....." was sent. It finished on the day that the full potential of that threat was made known (Hitler marching on Austria at 5.30 a.m. Moscow Time.

The Times of March 12, Page 11 reported

"The Prosecutor's Demands"
Death for all but two:

From a Special Correspondent,
Moscow March 11.

"Under the pitiless glare of 6 arc lamps, the prisoners filed into Court today to hear Vyshinsky's closing speech for the prosecution, which ended with a demand for the death penalty for all save Bessanoff and Rakovsky. They blinked, startled as they faced the light-batteries, and Rykoff and one or two others covered their faces with their hands as they stumbled to their seats, while two news reel cameras purred softly from the sides of the Court room.

The Prosecutor spoke for five hours, with one short interval, reading from a paper in a clear, monotonous voice, occasionally raised in indignation ....."

The Times goes on

"Thus fortified by history, Vyshinsky reverted to his main thesis that all members of the conspiracy were equally guilty, like a gang of bandits irrespective of individual action. Of Yagoda he said pithily: "If he had done a millionth part of what he actually did, he would still merit death."

In small degree, however, the Prosecutor belied himself by asking no more than 20 years imprisonment for Bessanoff, because

'he had acted principally as a go-between' and for Rakovsky because

'for the most part he held aloof from the rest of conspirators and was not directly involved in the dirtiest phases of the plot.'

Vyshinsky ended his speech as follows:

Shoot them like unclean dogs. Our country demands one thing: Crush these accursed reptiles.

Time will pass. The grave of these hated traitors will be overgrown with nettles and thistles, covered with the eternal contempt of all that is honest in the Soviet people. But the sun will shine again as before with its bright rays over us and our happy country.

Our country will go forward and forward along the path we have cleared of the last dirt and filth of the past.

Forward with great Stalin, our beloved leader and teacher.

Forward with Communism.

Times March 10 (Thursday) 1938:

Britain and Russia
Untrue Evidence at Moscow Trial,
Westminster, Wednesday

".....Two Labour members joined with two Unionists in putting questions to the Prime Minister today about the harm likely to be done to relations between this country and Soviet Russia by some evidence given at the Moscow Trial.

.....Mr. Chamberlain amid general cheers, declared that the allegations referred to were totally untrue."

This is one of the most important documents in history,

as important as Magna Carta was for good this has been for evil.

It led to the deaths of 55 million people in W.W. 2 with all its attendant suffering and evil, a war that is not yet concluded.

Chapter 11

The Merger

Surely some revelation is at hand,
Surely the Second Coming is at hand.
The Second Coming! Hardly are those words out
When a vast image out of Spiritus Mundi
Troubles my sight: somewhere in sands of the desert
A shape with lion body and the head of a man
A gaze blank and pitiless as the sun,
Is moving its slow thighs, while all about it
Reel shadows of the indignant desert birds.
The darkness drops again; but now I know
That twenty centuries of stony sleep
Were vexed to nightmare by a rocking cradle,
And what rough beast, its hour come round at last,
Slouches towards Betlehem to be born.

The Second Coming W.B. Yeats

The Media would have us believe there are two great Powers in the world, at each other's throats, War can break out between them at any time. They are the U.S. and the U.S.S.R.

The Conspirators have a number of plans to bring about the Merger of all peoples everywhere under their iron law. One is to break up the world into regions. Then you have regional government. Patriotism, called nationalism is then a nasty word. You become an internationalist. It's the in-thing. The best example is the Club of Rome. If we don't like some new law we are told there's nothing we can do about it; it's a directive from Brussels. President de Gaulle on the E.E.C. "That body of technocrats without a country, responsible to no one."

There are Regions in the making all over the world.

All the while the Big Powers were at each other's throats. Then they began to mellow. They began to talk and the people breathed a sigh of relief. There would be no nuclear war. They were having summits and smiling at each other. And what were they talking about? Peace of course. The Americans and the Europeans began to call Gorby the man of the decade, Gorby for President in the U.S. Wonderful, wonderful.

Gorbachev has written a book. The Harpur and Row English edition has this on the dustjacket:

> "The purpose of this book" says the author, "is to talk without intermediaries to the citizens of the whole world about things that, without exception, concern us all..... I am convinced that they, like me, worry about the future, of our planet."

The Hungarian edition of this same book has in the same place inside the dustjacket:

> "In our work and worries we are motivated by those Leninist ideals, and noble endeavours and goals which mobilised the workers of Russia seven decades ago to fight for the new happy world of Socialism. Perestroika is a continuation of the October Revolution."

And what were Lenin's ideals?

It was Lenin who wrote:

> "The lie is sacred, and deception will be our principal weapon."

He also explained that

> "The revolutionary dictatorship of the proletariat is power won and maintained by violence.....power that is unrestricted by any law."

He added that for this reason it does not matter that three-quarters of the world be destroyed provided that the remaining one-quarter be Communist.

Mr. Gorbachev, the Politbureau and the Central Committee of the Communist Party are all professed followers of Lenin's philosophy.

If Gorbachev's Perestroika doesn't work according to plan, he may have to go, though he's the best P.R. man they've ever had, but if he does, it will not be the Politbureau or the Central Committee of the Communist Party that will send him packing, though they may issue the order. **"They"** will decide.

Working towards World Government via the Regional Plan has been having some headaches, especially in the U.S. where the people like having their individual states being left with some local power, so a grand idea began to take shape, an idea that would appeal to every man black, white and brown. Mother Earth was in danger. We must all unite to save Mother Earth from the Greenhouse effect, the ozone hole, and toxic pollution. This terrible menace facing us all must be tackled. This leads to conferences sometimes convened by film stars where everyone looks very serious. There are scientists, film makers, authors, artists, and environmentalists all giving serious attention to protecting you and me from our own negligence. Mother Earth has to be saved so there's no time now for narrow nationalistic feelings, racial pride, patriotism, ethnic differences, competing cultural traditions, religious beliefs or economic and financial problems.

There's yet another way towards World Government. There's the Bildeburgers, a highly secret society engaged, we are told, in solving our financial problems which of course they have no hand in creating. Then there's the Trilateral Commission made up of Big Business Men from the U.S., Western Europe and Japan. When any of these secret societies meet three layers of security surround their meeting place, the press is kept out and if any statement is issued it is about how hard they are working to bring us peace and happiness.

When Ronald Reagan was going for the Presidency of the U.S. and patriotic Americans were beginning to fight back for their country Reagan promised he would never run with any member of the Trilateral Commission. But soon he had to forget his promise and accept Mr. George Bush, not only a Trilateralist but a member of a highly Secret Society known as The Order on which Professor Anthony Sutton has written a whole book.

Since the Trilaterlists represent Big Business, made up of what has come to be called Multi-Nationals, it is expected that the Multi-National will lead the way to the Big Merger. But first there are a number of State sponsored companies running very successful businesses. We have Aer Lingus and many others. These are to be privatised. In Britain water has been privatised, but did the man in the street get any shares. Ask him. Now how come that this idea of privatisation all happened to spring up simultaneously in Britain, Ireland, Australia and other far-away places. Would such a thing have been made to happen.

The Berlin Wall and The Iron Curtain have come down and now there's a glorious chance for the multi-nationals to move in. They will show the people of Eastern Europe how to put bread and meat on the table, and they will be very grateful for a square meal at last, but ultimately will they have that precious thing called freedom. Is it in the blueprint? Not if we heed the warnings of George Orwell as he tried to reach us in his Animal Farm and '1984'. In the parable of the rich man and Lazarus, Our Lord warned us that even if the Rich Man were to come back from the dead he would not be heeded. If they wouldn't heed the Prophets they would not believe someone back from the dead.

People control can go by many fancy names. Thomas

106

James Norton in "Undermining the Constitution" (1950) says:

> *"As big a thing as the great American Republic could not have been put on the skids without years of steady work. Beginning with 1933, Socialism (control by government of production, distribution and exchange), Fascism (Socialism by Corporations), and Communism (confiscation by government of private property through graduated taxes and the abolition of inheritance), all forbidden by the Constitution because in no way authorised, and in many ways condemned by implication, spread with the rapidity of a fire on the prairie. But the seizure by them of the liberty and property of Americans began before 1933."*

But trying to establish corporate socialism as an accepted form of government in the 1930's was attempting "to do too much too soon" according to one of their own.

Fascism and Nazism were defeated in World War II to make the world safe for their socialist sisters: Communism in the East and Fabianism in the West. In the West corporate socialsim was to be given a new name with no stigma, supported by the World Bank and the IMF. Pre-war in Germany and Italy the Government controlled the corporations. Under today's system the corporations control the government. And as The Don Bell Reports (P.O. 2223 Palm Beach Fr. 3340):

> *"If an economic merger between the U.S. and the U.S.S.R. is to be accomplished, the U.S.S.R. must relax its absolute control over the 'republics' and satellites. It must allow them to assume a state of seeming independence, as in Poland and Hungary. It must let the various trade groups know as councils, ministries, soviets, etc. work as corporations work in the West. These trade groups*

acting as corporations must be allowed to plan production, quality, prices, distribution, labour standards, etc. on their own but, of course, under Supreme Soviet supervision. And this is exactly what Gorbachev is trying to accomplish through Perestroika."

Economic merger must come before political merger is possible in the building of the super state.

The Commies and the Cappies
In confrontation play
These innimical chappies
At last call it a day;
The name calling, the spying
And armaments galore
Now suddenly are vying
For who loves whom the more.

B.E. Biggs.

CHAPTER 12

The Woman of Genesis

Who is she that cometh forth as the morning rising,
Fair as the Moon, bright as the sun,
Terrible as an army in battle array.

From the Magnificat.

The war began in Eden when God said "I will put enmity between thee and the Woman." Up to this point an account has been given of the war as it has been waged by the serpent.

The 16th century witnessed the great split in the Church. It was then, 1531, Our Lady came to Mexico, leaving there a picture of herself standing on the serpent which became known as Our Lady of Quadalupe. In Mexico at that time as many as 8,000 men would be offered in human sacrifice in one day to Pagan Gods. Following Mary's appearance there, eight million converted to Catholocism in just three years. The pagan temples were gone forever.

In 1830 Mary came to Paris to a nun in the Convent of the Sisters of Charity in the Rue du Bac. There she told the history of France up to the time of the Commune in 1870, if men did not repent of their sins. She asked that a medal be struck which came to be known as The Miraculous Medal because of the many miracles performed through its use. As in Mexico the front of the medal shows Mary standing on the head of the serpent surrounded by the inscription: "O Mary conceived without sin, pray for us who have recourse to thee." The doctrine of the Immaculate Conception was not infallibly defined until 1854. The back of the medal shows that M for Maria is inextricably bound up with the realities unfolding at the foot of the Cross, where there are two hearts, one of which is pierced with a sword. "And thine own soul a sword shall pierce." Simeon at the Presentation in the Temple.

"For the Word of God is living and active and more piercing than any two edged sword."

Heb. 4:12.

"And from his mouth came out a sharp two edged sword."

Rev. 1:16.

"And the Seed is the Word of God."

Luke 8:12.

St. Augustine describes Calvary as a Mystical Marriage of the Word with the Woman. He says:

"Christ went forth from His Heavenly mansions to the field of the Cross,

And there mounting it, consummated his marriage,

It was bed not of joy but of pain,

And he lovingly gave himself up to the Woman forever."

Fulton Sheen describes the water and blood issuing from the side of Christ as mystical seminal fluid.

The Mystical Marriage consummated at Calvary between the Word and the Woman has as its issue John at the foot of the Cross. This mystic conception, as in the physical conception of Jesus, is by perception. "The Angel of the Lord declared unto Mary, and she conceived of the Holy Spirit." The Angelus.

There is a distinction in Scripture between the Word of God being alive and active. Heb. 4:2. Between Calvary and Pentecost the divine fecundity is preserved alive in John alone. At Pentecost this divine fecundity is disseminated by the Holy Spirit among those who like Jesus had been ritually cleansed by the waters of the Baptist.

We see this symbolised in Catholic ritual in a darkened Church on Easter Saturday night when the waters are fructified by the immersion of a lighted candle.

From the Mystical standpoint John is to the Mystical Body of Christ what the gene is to the species in the natural order. In the Mystical order it is then through John there is effected the fecundity transference from the Word.

The masonic ritual of the Rose Croix (18th degree) is the profane and phallic mimicry of the fecundity transference. The doctrine of the point within a circle surmounted by a book and encompassed by the two St. Johns (claimed by Masonry as its Patrons) denotes in mimicry the dissemination of the fecundity of the Word among those ritually initiated.

We see here two interpretations of **the same central event of cosmic history.** One sees 'Divinity as Person', the other, the profane, sees 'Divinity as Principle'. Since these two systems of Divinity are embodied in institutions that are the declared enemies of each other it behoves us to enquire what plane of combat would equally lend itself to both. Should such a plane of combat exist it also behoves us to seek within it a Priesthood that is claimed by both. Here it is well to call to mind Rakovsky's referring to the 'Divinity as Principle' system of Baruch Spinosa as being but a version adequate to the particular epoch of **"Their"** philosophy, which he said was a much earlier one, standing on a much higher level. The earliest and highest priesthood (claimed by Divinity as Person') is the high Priesthood of Melchisedech.

The Rose Croix 18th Degree of Masonry has the Melchisedech Priesthood incorporated within it. In as much as Melchisedech may be considered as both Person and Principle (Heb. 7:3) the Order of Melchisedech equally lends itself as a plane of combat for those rival systems of Divinity that have been martially equilibrated in Gen. 3:15.

The primal thesis of Lucifer in the Garden of Eden was that Divinity is a Principle.

At Lourdes in 1858, four years after the dogma of the Immaculate conception had been infallibly defined, the Woman appeared to a girl called Bernadette. On being questioned as to who she was, she replied: "I am the Immaculate Conception." Bernadette, being unlettered, did not know what either word meant. Again the woman asked for prayers and penance so that men might be saved from their sins.

At the time when the Supreme Pontiff of Masonry, Albert Pike, was preparing his Instructions, a vision appeared on the gable end wall of a little Church in Knock, Ireland. Pike's instructions were issued to the 23 Supreme Councils of the World and have been recorded by A.C. De La Rive in La Femme et L'Enfant dans la France - Maconnerie Universelle (P. 588) from which we translate and quote:

"That which we must say to the crowd is - We worship a God, but it is the God that one adores without superstition.

To you, Sovereign Grand Inspectors General, we say this, that you may repeat it to the Brethern of the 32nd, 31st and 30th degrees - The Masonic religion should be, by all of us initiates of the high degrees, maintained in the purity of the Luciferian doctrine."

Pike went on to say that there were two Gods, one good and one bad. The good was, of course, Lucifer, and the bad the God of the Christians. This gem of wisdom is told only to the higher initiates. All lesser brethren are told that God is a principle, the principle of fructification, that it is in all nature, and that each and every one of us is part of it. We are all divine and evolving towards the omega point. This will be Heaven and we'll all be there. Pike goes on:

"Thus the universe is balanced by two forces which maintain its **equilibrium**; the force of attraction and that of repulsion. These two forces exist in physics, philosophy and religion. And the scientific reality of the divine dualism is demonstrated by the phenomena of polarity and by the universal law of sympathies and antipathies....

Lucifer, God of Light and God of Good, is struggling for humanity against Adonay, the God of Darkness and Evil."

Here is quoted just one of the Instructions:

"To be able, at will, to use or to abstain, is a twofold power. Woman fetters thee by thy desires, we say to the adept, well, use women often and without passion; thou wilt thus become master of thy desires, and thou wilt enchain woman. From which it must perforce result that the real Mason will succeed in easily solving the problem of the flesh."

Knock

The gable end wall of the Church at Knock was lit up by a bright light for two hours from 7 p.m. to 9 p.m. on the evening of the 21 August 1879, eve of Mary's feast day. At the centre of the vision was a table or altar, on which stood a live lamb about six weeks old. Rising above the lamb was a cross and all around were angels wrapt in adoration. A little to the left of the altar stood St. John, the Evangelist, holding a missal, with his right hand raised, the first and second fingers pointing upwards as if preaching. Slightly to the left of St. John stood Our Lady, looking towards Heaven, as if in ecstasy, her hands raised. Next to Our Lady stood St. Joseph, head bowed in prayer.

The vision represented Calvary and the Mass, one and the same **cosmic event**, the Mass being Calvary outside of time and space. The whole was surrounded by a heavenly light, the light of Heaven confronting the darkness of Masonry. No word was spoken. There was no need. The Fall was redeemed by the Lamb of God, seen live on the altar, at the gable end of this humble wayside Church.

Great numbers of people saw the vision. Fifty years later a Commission studied the vision. Fifteen people still alive gave sworn statements describing what they had seen. The fifteen were scattered far and wide, some in America. All gave the exact same description of the vision.

Fatima

Fatima was next. Fatima is a small town in the north of Portugal. Three children, Lucia aged 10, Francisco aged 9, and his sister aged 7, minded sheep at a place called the Cova for their families. In 1916 an angel appeared to them on three occasions. He told them he was the Guardian angel of Portugal, that God had designs on them and he taught them how to pray.

It was 13 May, 1917, at 12 noon the children were playing, when suddenly they were startled by what appeared to be a flash of lightening. Then they saw a beautiful lady dressed in white, poised over a holm oak sapling. She was more brilliant than the sun, radiating a sparkling light. The Lady spoke:

"Do not be afraid. I will do you no harm. I am from Heaven and I have come to ask you to come here for six months on the 13th day at the same time. Later on I will tell you what I want and I will return here a seventh time."

Lucia asked some questions, if they would go to Heaven, and about some people who had died in recent times. Yes, they were in Heaven and one was in Purgatory. Our Lady asked the children:

"Do you wish to offer up to God all the sufferings He desires to send you in reparation for the sins by which he is offended and in supplication for the conversion of sinners?"

When the children replied: "Yes, we do," Our

114

*Lady said: "Then you will have much to suffer, but
the grace of God will comfort you."*
Finally our Lady instructed the children:
*"Say the Rosary every day in order to obtain
peace for the world and the end of the war."*

Our Lady duly appeared in June when she promised to take Jacinto and Francisco to Heaven soon. Francisco died in 1919 and Jacinto in 1920, both having suffered gladly a great deal for the conversion of sinners.

The 13th July, 1917, will stand out as one of the most momentous days in history, for on that day Our Lady prophesied the history of the world down to the present day. She asked the children to pray for the conversion of sinners and to say:

*"Oh Jesus this is for the love of you, for the
conversion of sinners, and in reparation for the
sins committed against the Immaculate Heart of
Mary."*

Then the children were given a vision of Hell in which they could see demons and those who were damned. Lucia cried out in terror calling upon Our Lady.

*"We could see a vast sea of fire," she revealed
many years later. "Plunged in the flames were
demons and lost souls, as if they were red hot coals,
transparent and black or bronze-coloured, in
human form, which floated about in the
conflagration, borne by the flames which issued
from them, with clouds of smoke falling on all sides
as sparks fall into a great conflagration without
weight or equilibrium, amid shrieks and groans of
sorrow and despair that horrified us and caused us
to tremble with fear. The devils could be
distinguished by horrible and loathsome forms of*

*animals, frightful and unknown, but transparent
like black coals that have turned red-hot."*

Full of fear, the children raised their eyes beseechingly to
the Lady who said to them, with unspeakable sadness and tenderness:

*"You saw Hell where the souls of poor sinners
go. In order to save them, God wishes to establish
in the world devotion to my Immaculate Heart. If
people do what I ask many souls will be saved and
there will be peace. The war is going to end. But
if people do not stop offending God, another, even
worse, will begin in the reign of Pius XI. When you
see a night illuminated by an unknown light, know
that it is the great sign that God gives you that he
is going to punish the world by means of war,
hunger and persecution of the Church and of the
Holy Father. To prevent it, I will come to ask for
the consecration of Russia to my Immaculate Heart
and the Communion of reparation on the first
Saturdays. If people attend to my requests, Russia
will be converted and the world will have peace. If
not, Russia will spread its errors throughout the
world, fomenting wars and persecutions of the
Church. The good will be martyred, the Holy
Father will have much to suffer, and various nations
will be annihilated. In the end, my Immaculate
Heart will triumph. The Holy Father will consecrate
Russia to me; it will be converted, and a certain
period of peace will be granted to the world. In
Portugal the dogmas of the Faith will always be
kept...."*

(Here follows the third secret which has never been
revealed).

116

Lucia had asked for a miracle and Our Lady promised it. The miracle of the sun on 13 October, 1917, was the great heavenly sign given by God to confirm the reality of the divine intervention at Fatima and the seriousness of His message for mankind. The children had told of the promise, which spread through Portugal like a prairie fire and was splashed across the pages of the anti-clerical press. As far as is known, for the very first time in history, a prophet or seer was asking all the people to assemble at a certain place and time to witness a public miracle to prove that the message which had been received came from God. The revolutionary Government, which had vowed to stamp out religion in two generations, were taking no chances with what they regarded as sheer religious fanaticism. Armed soldiers were sent to the Cova on the morning of the 13 October to prevent people gathering there. The press lampooned the whole affair. Yet despite the armed guards, and appalling weather conditions, 70,000 people gathered at the Cova.

This was only the third time in history that God had used the sun to perform a miracle - the other two occasions being the prolongation of daylight at the prayer of Joshua (Joshua 10), and the sign given to the King of Judah in 714 B.C. by the prophet Ezekiel in which the shadow of a sundial retraced its path by ten hours (Kings 4:20). But what made the Fatima miracle unique was that its exact time and location were publicly announced months beforehand. Some of the most eloquent descriptions of what happened have been given by reporters for the secular press who came to scoff. Only the most brief description can be given here. According to the testimony of thousands present there, the sun appeared like a dull silver plate spinning round in a circular movement as if it were moved by electricity. On the faces of the people an expression of ecstatic rapture could be observed. The sun neither burned nor blinded their eyes. According to Diario de Noticias (Daily News) of 15 October 1917:

> *"Before the astonished eyes of the crowd, whose aspect was biblical, as they stood bareheaded, pale with fright, eagerly searching the sky, the sun trembled, made sudden incredible movements outside all cosmic laws - the sun 'danced' according to the typical expression of the people."*

It then left its orbit in the sky and came whirling toward the earth almost touching it. That great mass of seventy thousand people fell to its knees crying out for mercy, thinking it was the end of the world. The whole episode lasted roughly twelve minutes, quite a long time to watch a cosmic display that the people believed was about to be the end of the world. Then suddenly the sky was swept clear of clouds and the sun followed its course in its usual splendour, so that no one ventured to gaze at it directly.

Prior to the miracle the children had spoken to Our Lady who was accompanied by St. Joseph and the Divine Infant.

On the 13 July, 1917, Our Lady said the Second World War, worse than the one then raging, would begin in the reign of Pius XI. Pius XI did not become Pope until 1922, and in 1917, it could not be known that there would ever be a Pope who would be called Pius XI. World War II actually began with the invasion of Austria while Pius XI still reigned, as did the Spanish Civil War, being essentially a war against God in which untold numbers of churches were destroyed, 14 Bishops and 7,000 priests and religious were martyred. The anti-God nature of the conflict was epitomised by the 'execution' by a firing squad of the famous granite statue of the Sacred Heart in the geographical centre of Spain.

The unknown light, which was to be the "great sign" given by God that the punishment of the world was at hand, got extensive coverage in the national press in every country; the New York Times accorded it almost an entire page. Following its appearance Lucia wrote to the Cardinal Patriarch of Lisbon to this effect:

"War is imminent. The sins of men will be washed in their own blood. Those nations will suffer most in the war which tried to destroy the Kingdom of God. Portugal will suffer some of the consequences of the war, but because of our country's consecration to the Immaculate Heart, she will not suffer them all."

(See Fatima: The Great Sign by Francis Johnston, P.39.)

At Fatima, Our Lady asked for the following in order to bring peace to the world:

1. The daily recitation of the Rosary.
2. The offering of one's daily duties, well done, to God as a sacrifice.
3. The wearing of the Brown Scapular.
4. Confession, Mass and Holy Communion on the First Saturday of the month.
5. Finally, the consecration of Russia to the Immaculate Heart of Mary, by the Pope, in union with all the Bishops of the world on the same day. This has not as yet been done at the date of writing early 1990.

Our Lady said at Fatima that war was a punishment for sin. Since 1917 many of the worst sins have become legalised in nearly every country in the world, principally that of abortion which is mass murder. This is made possible by the great apostasy which we see before our eyes, and which is believed by many students of the Fatima message to be the subject of the Third Secret of Fatima, never revealed.

That people will be richly rewarded for carrying out the wishes of Our Mother at Fatima was revealed when the atom bomb was dropped in Hiroshima. There, six Jesuits were living the Message of Fatima, and though they were right in the heart of the place where the bomb fell, not one of them got the slightest scratch. All around them 100,000 were killed instantly, and another 100,000 were badly burned. The Church of St. Maximilian Kolbe was also left untouched, though in the centre of the slaughter.

The Second World War has never officially ended, since no peace treaty has been signed. Only divine intervention can bring peace to the world now or in the future. When ten per cent of the people of Austria were saying the daily Rosary the Soviet Army marched voluntarily out of the country.

The vision of Hell had the greatest impact on little Jacinta. At the thought of the red raging flames and the terrifying sight and sound of millions of lost souls she would wail, wringing her hands:

"Oh Hell, Oh, Hell! Mother of God have pity on those who do not amend their lives. If men only knew what awaits them in eternity, they would do everything in their power to change their lives."

Frequently she would call to her brother, Francisco, saying: "Are you praying with me? We must pray very much to save souls from Hell. So many go there, so many."

At other times she would ask Lucia: "Why doesn't Our Lady show Hell to sinners? If only they saw it, they would never commit sins again." On one occasion she said to Lucia: "Look, I am going to Heaven soon, but you are to stay here. If Our Lady lets you, tell everyone what Hell is like so that they won't sin anymore and not go there."

The three children undertook the most severe penances for the salvation of sinners. They gave their lunches to the poor, even to the sheep; they didn't drink during the furnace-like heat of August, 1917 - an almost unendurable penance, especially for children. They also responded readily to Our Lady's request for prayer, spending long hours on their knees under a blistering sun, reciting the rosary and the Angel's prayer, over and over again: In a letter to a nephew (a Salesian priest) Lucia stressed the need for prayer, saying among much else: "It is sad that so many are allowing themselves to be dominated by the diabolical wave that is sweeping the world, and they are so blind that they cannot see their error.... Never consider the time wasted that you spend in prayer. You will discover that in prayer, God communicates to you the light, strength and grace you need to do all He expects of you..... Let time be lacking for everything else, but never for prayer." (Quoted in Soul Magazine, November - December 1976).

In 1966 the communists were so sure of seizing power in Brazil the Party Secretary announced to the Moscow International Press the precise day (a few weeks hence) when the hammer and sickle would fly over that vast strategic country. "All key positions were in the hands of notorious communists or pro-communists," recalled Fr. Valerio Alberton, S.J. Vice-Director of the National Federation of Marian Congregations of Brazil.

"The penetration went deep into even Catholic
Faculties. Communist cells were discovered even
in our colleges. Neither did Catholic Associations
escape. It was terrible."

At the eleventh hour a nation-wide rosary crusade was launched; millions implored the Immaculate heart of Mary to save them. An immense gathering of 800,000 women marched through the centre of Sao Paulo, praying the rosary for three

121

hours. "Mother of God," they cried, "preserve us from the fate and suffering of the martyred women of Cuba, Poland, Hungary and other enslaved nations." Similar scenes were witnessed in other cities. The communist President Goulart, seeing the vast groundswell against him, fled the country. The red shadow over Brazil lifted.

The experience was repeated in Portugal in 1975. The Portuguese people went down on their knees and prayed the rosary as never before, entreating Our Lady of Fatima to save them. The prayer-storm reached its climax on 13 October 1975. Weeks later, the long expected communist coup was almost bloodlessly and decisively crushed. At the 8th Fatima Congress at Kevelaer, Germany, on 18 September 1977 the Cardinal Patriarch of Lisbon proclaimed:

"I can say that it was the consecration of Portugal made in Fatima to the Immaculate Heart of Mary by the Portuguese bishops in 1931 and 1938 that defended Portugal from the common peril....."

A final example occured in Chile. The communist government of Dr. Allende was over thrown by a three-year rosary and scapular campaign, and one of the first acts of the new government was to rebuild the national shrine of Our Lady of Mount Carmel. The present system may leave a lot to be desired but is a long way better than Orwell's Animal Farm way of life.

In this Cosmic War we ordinary people are the foot soldiers of Christ and the Woman, joined in a Mystical Marriage at Calvary. We are the Mystical issue and we were promised victory in Gen. 3.15.

Postscript

There is a French proverb which says the more things change the more they remain the same. This describes exactly what is happening in Eastern Europe today. There is going to be no real freedom, just enough to beguile people that it is real. The reader is urged to go back and read Rakovsky many times. He was talking about world history going back centuries and into the future - unless the humasn race as a whole now amends its' ways. Rakovsky did not take into account that at the dawn of history the serpent was told the Woman would crush his head and that he would lie in wait for her heel. The woman will crush his head when enough human beings cooperate with her by amending their lives and doing what she asked at Fatima In this context I would apeal to my fellow countrymen in Northern Ireland. Do you not see that you are puppets on a string manipulated by **"Them"**, as are those you believe are your enemies. I would ask you to read again extracts from the chapter on Psychopolitics. Are you sure you are not under the spell of some psychopolitician. While you continue the violence there will be no winner only **"They"**. **"They"** will go on winning and supplying you with arms and see that you have money.

Professor Carroll Quigley in his monumental work "Tragedy and Hope" says:

> " The Western Civilisation is coming to a decline as twelve others did before us. We are going to displace capital, divert wealth and energies from production to non-production activities. We are reducing our civilisation through birth control and abortion. We are decaying from within".

A major instrument of that decay is the Government Debt of every country. Government Debt is an absurdity, in

Rakovsky"s words an abstraction. As much as ninety-eight per cent of it made with paper and ink from nothing. It is a costless entry in a leger, but the taxpayer pays a slave tax on it, the same as if it were real.

Despite the power and venom of the enemy there are many signs that Ireland can turn back this tide of evil that is threatening to engulf us.

The Lord works through little people. Fortunately we have a great number of little people who have the capacity to topple the Goliaths. They are the small farmer, the small everybody. Hold onto your small farm, your small home. **"They"** are after it, as **"They"** are after your children.

Fight and pray, the Lord has promised you victory.
Gen. 3;15

Bibliography

AMERICA:

None Dare Call It Conspiracy, Concord Press, Seal Beach, California.

Nine Men Against America, Rosalie M. Gordon, Western Islands, Belmont Massachusetts.

Will America Surrender?, Slodoban M. Draskovich, Devin-Adair, Old Greenwich, Connecticut.

The Lattimore Story, John T. Flynn, Devin-Adair, Old Greenwich, Connecticut.

The Roosevelt Myth, John T. Flynn, Devin-Adair, Old Greenwich, Connecticut.

National Suicide: Military Aid to the Soviet Union, Anthony C.Sutton, Arlington House, New Rochelle, New York.

Hell's War Against Our Children, John O' Connor O.P., Saint Raphael's Productions, Quebec Canada

CHRISTIANITY:

The Workers' Charter, Pope Leo XIII, Catholic Truth Society, London, England.

The Social Order, Pope Pius XI, Catholic Truth Society, London, England.

Atheistic Communism, Pope Pius XI, Catholic Truth Society, London, England.

Marriage and the Moral Law, Pope Pius XII, Catholic Truth Society, London, England.

The Kingship of Christ and Organized Naturalism, Rev. Denis Fahey, Regina Publications, Dublin, Ireland.

A History of the Protestant Reformation in England and Ireland, William Cobbett, London, England (1854-5).

The Mystical Body of Christ in the Modern World, Fr. Denis Fahey, C.SS.

125

The Mystical Body of Christ and The Reorganisation of Society, Fr. Denis Fahey, C.SS.

Money Manipulation and Social Order, Y.P. House, Parnell Square, Dublin.

Freemasonry & The Anti-Christian Movement, Rev. E. Cahill, S.J., M.H. Gill & Son, Dublin.

History of the Protestant Reformation, Cobbett, P.O. Box 542, Stratford, Conn. 06497.

Evidence of Satan in the Modern World, Leon Cristiani, TAN, Rockford, Ill. 61105.

Humanistic Morals & Values Education, Vince Nesbitt, 12 Beta Road Lane Cove, N.S.W. 2066, Australia.

Cranmer's Godly Order, Michael Davies, Augustine Publishing Co., Devon.

The Church Since Vatican II, Michael Davies, Augustine Publishing Co., Devon.

N.E.A. Trojan Horse in American Education, Samuel L. Blemenfeld.

John Paul II and the Battle for Vatican II, Richard Cowden-Guido, Trinity Communications, Manassis Virginia.

COMMUNISM:

Biographical Dictionary of the Left, Francis X. Gannon, Western Islands, Belmont, Massachusets.

"We Will Bury You", ed. Brian Crozier, Tom Stacey Ltd., London, England.

The Assault on the West, Ian Greig, Foreign Affairs Publishing Co. Ltd., Petersham, Surrey, England.

Western Technology and Soviet Economic Development, Anthony C. Sutton, Hoover Institution Press, Stanford, California

The Rulers of Russia, Rev. Dennis Fahey, Regina Publications, Dublin, Ireland.

You Can Trust the Communists (to be Communists), Fred Schwarz, Christian Anti-Communism Crusade, Long Beach, California.

Solshenitsyn at Harvard, Ethics and Public Policy Centre, Washington, D.C.

Operation Keelhaul: The Story of Forced Repatriation from 1944 to the Present, Devin-Adair, Old Greenwich, Connecticut.

I Was a Slave in Russia, John Noble, Devin-Adair, Old Greenwich, Connecticut.

Communism, Conspiracy and Treason, KRP Publications, London, England.

The Fabian Socialist Contribution to the Communist Advance, Eric D. Butler, Australia League of Rights, Melbourne.

Black on Red, Robert Robinson, Acropolis Books Ltd.Washington D.C.

CONSPIRACY:

The Banker's Conspiracy, Arthur Kitson, London Elliot Stock, 16/17 Paternoster Row, E.C.

Proofs of a Conspiracy, John Robison, Western Islands, Los Angeles.

Tearing Away the Veils (The Financiers who Control the World) Francois Coty, P.O. 216, Hawthorne CA.

This Age of Conflict, Ivor Benson, Dolphin Press Ltd., CA.

The World Order, Eustace Mullins, P.O. Box 1105 Staunton, CA. 24401.

The War Called Peace, The Soviet Peace Offensive, Western Goals, 309A Cameron Street, Alexandria, Va. 22314.

Victory Denied, Why Your Son Faces Death in "No-Win Wars", Major A.E. Roberts Committee to Restore the Constitution, Fort Collins, Colo, 80521.

The Invisible Government, Dan Smoot, Irish Home Library, P.O. 1547, Rathmines Dublin.

Why Has the Country Not Been Told? The Soviet "War Beneath the Level of Military Conflict", Commander M.J.L. Blake, R.N., Col. B.S. Turner, C.Eng. M.I. Mech., E. Bloomfield Books, Suffolk, England.

The Aids Cover-Up, Gene Antonio, Ignatius Press, San Francisco.

Behind The Lodge Door, Paul A. Fisher, Shield Publishing Inc., Washington D.C.

The Rockefeller File - Secret, Gary Allen, '76 Press, Seal Beach, CA.

The Hidden Dangers of the Rainbow, Coustmer Cousby.

ECONOMICS :

Money, Manipulation and Social Order, Rev. Denis Fahey, Regina Publications, Dublin.

Wealth, Virtual Wealth and Debt, Frederick Soddy, Omni Publications, Hawthorne, California.

Dividing the Wealth: Are You Getting Your Share? Howard E. Kershner, Devin-Adair, Old Greenwich, Connecticut.

Foundations and Tax-Free Cash, Gary Allen and Harold Lord Varney, American Opinion, Belmont, Massachusetts.

The Anti-Capitalistic Mentality, Ludwig von Mises, Libertarian Press, South Holland, Illinois.

Elements of Social Credit, Social Credit Secretariat, Liverpool, England (1946).

Economic Democracy, C.H. Douglas, Omni Publications, Hawthorne, California.

EVOLUTION:

The Crumbling Theory of Evolution, J.W.G. Johnson, 1132 Waterworkds Rd., The Gap. Q. 4061, Australia.

The Evolution Hoax Exposed (former Title: Why Colleges Breed Communists), A.N. Field, Tan Books Inc., Rockford, I11. 65505.

Evolution (The Fossils Say NO!) Duane T. Gish, PH.D., Creation Life Pub., San Dieg.

GERMANY AND JAPAN:

Wall Street and the Rise of Hitler, Antony C. Sutton, Bloomfield Books, Sudbury, Suffolk, England.

"Oil, Deviance and the Traditional World Order - Japanese and German Strategies for Violent Change 1931-41", John M.W. Chapman, Chap. 19 in Tradition and Modern Japan, Paul Norbury Publications, Tenterden, Kent, England.

France The Tragic years, Sisley Huddleston, Western Islands, Belmont, Massachusetts.

MISCELLANEOUS:

You're Next on the List, David O. Woodbury, Western Islands, Belmont, Massachusetts.

The Whole of their Lives, Benjamin Gitlow, Western Islands, Belmont, Massachusetts.

Waters Flowing East, Elizabeth Fry, Britons Publishing Co.

The Federal Reserve Bank, H.S. Kenan, The Noontide Press, Los Angeles, California.

Tortured for Christ, Richard Wurmbrand, Hodder & Stoughton, London.

1984, George Orwell, published by Penguin Books.

REVOLUTION:

World Revolution (The Plot against Civilization) Nesta II. Webster, Constable & Co., London.

Pawns in the Game, William Guy Carr, Angriff Press, Box 2726, Hollywood Ca. 90028.

Red Fog Over America, William Guy Carr, Angriff Press, Box 2726, Hollywood Ca. 90028.

Workers' Paradise Lost, Eugene Lyons

Fifty Years of Soviet Communism: A balance Sheet, Eugene Lyons, Paperback Library Inc., New York.

The Unseen Hand (An Introduction to the Conspiratorial View of History) A. Ralph Epperson, Publius Press 3100 So. Philamena Pl. Tucson, Ar. 85730.

Karl Marx :True Or False Prophet? Deirdre Manifold, Firinne Press, 15 Dalysfort Road, Galway.

Fabian Freeway, Rose L. Martin, *High Road to Socialism in the U.S.A.* Rose L. Martin, Fidelis Pub. Inc., P.O. Box 1338, Santa Monica, CA. 90406.

The Case of Tyler Kent, John Howland Snow, The Long House, P.O. Box 3, New Canaan, Conn. 06840.

The Red Pattern of World Conquest, Eric D. Butler, Intelligence Pub. 65, Craddocks Ave., Ashtead, Surrey, G.B.

None Dare Call It Treason, John A. Stormer, Liberty Bell Press, P.O. Box 32, Foorissant, Mi.

The Actor, A Study in Deception, The True Story of John Foster Dulles. Alan Stang Western Islands Pub., Boston.

This Was My Choice, Igor Gouzenko, Palm Pub., Montreal.

UNITED NATIONS:

The United Nations Conspiracy, Robert W. Lee, Western Islands, Belmont, Massachusetts.

Red Spies in the UN, Pierre J. Huss and George Carpozi, Coward-McCann, New York.

The Fearful Master: A Second Look at the UN, G. Edward Griffin, Western Islands, Belmont, Massachusetts.

Manacles for Mankind, Mark Ewell, Britons Publishing Co., London.

Books by Firinne

Fatima and the Great Conspiracy by Deirdre Manifold

Karl Marx, True or False Prophet by Deirdre Manifold

Blessed Margaret of Castello - Heroine of the Unwanted
    by Deirdre Manifold

Origin of the Present Day Problems in the Catholic Church
    by Rev. Paul A. Wickens

A Primary Catechism - Based on the Old Penny
    by Sr. Francis Mc Andrew S.J.C.

Our Catholic Faith - A Doctrine Book for First Years
    by Sr. Francis Mc Andrew S.J.C.